Towards The Sunrise

Pen Portraits of Some of the Unnamed Women of the Bible

by
Pauline Lewis

MOORLEY'S Print & Publishing

British Library Cataloguing in Publication Data.
A catalogue record for this book is available
from the British Library.

ISBN 0 86071 559 0

MOORLEY'S Print & Publishing
23 Park Rd., Ilkeston, Derbys DE7 5DA
Tel/Fax: (0115) 932 0643

CONTENTS

INTRODUCTION

It has been a Christian tradition throughout the centuries to bury our dead facing east, in glorious hope of the coming of the Son of Man and resurrection morn. It is good to be buried in hope, but how much better to live our lives 'towards the sunrise.'

I love the references in the Old Testament, where it defines the east as 'towards the sunrise.' The Bible names many of the men and women of faith who not only died, but lived in faith, their faces turned towards the sunrise, but there are others too whose names are not given. I have written of these unnamed yet very real people and trust that as we hear the old stories told through their eyes that we will find inspiration.

Like them, we may never have our names recorded among the wise or famous, but we too can live and die, towards the sunrise.

MOORLEY'S

We are growing publishers, adding several new titles to our list each year. We also undertake private publications and commissioned works.

Our range of publications includes:

Books of Verse:
Devotional Poetry
Recitations
Drama
Bible Plays
Sketches
Nativity Plays
Passiontide Plays
Easter Plays
Demonstrations
Resource Books
Assembly Material
Songs and Musicals
Children's Addresses
Prayers and Graces
Daily Readings
Books for Speakers
Activity Books
Quizzes
Puzzles
Painting Books
Church Stationery
Notice Books
Cradle Rolls
Hymn Board Numbers

Please send a stamped addressed envelope (approx. 9" x 6") for the current catalogue or consult your local Christian Bookshop who should stock or be able to order our titles.

CHAPTER 1

BOOKED FOR A WORLD CRUISE
Genesis chapters 6 - 8

She was booked for a world cruise, even before ships, let alone navigation had been invented. There were only eight of them in the end who sailed, and yet her name is not even mentioned on the passenger list. The only record we have of this woman is that she was someone's wife. Her name seems to have been of no importance, yet her life was of great significance, because she was saved, and without her there would be no human race as we know it.

Come to think of it, it is only Noah's name that is recorded. It says that Noah and his wife, and his sons and their wives entered into the ark. We had already been told the names of those sons but not of their wives.

What was her life like, this woman whose name seems to be not worth mentioning? We know that she lived in a time of sliding standards, when immorality was rife. Yes, they were still marrying and giving in marriage. It could have been that she was promised in marriage when she was yet a child, but she was fortunate to ever have a husband, for there was so much violence in the land where she lived and there must have been a protecting hand on her that she was not raped or abducted.

Of course, she could have married Shem before Noah had his call, but it is unlikely, for Noah was five hundred before he started his family, and it was at this time that God spoke to him, commanding him to build this great ship that was to be the means of their salvation.

We imagine that, even as a young girl, she would have known of this young man that she was eventually to marry for he was different, he and his brothers and his father. Everyone was talking about them, laughing and mocking, that they should dare to believe that there was a God who cared about how they lived, who wanted them to live clean and upright lives and who was coming in judgment to cleanse the earth and to wash away those who were violating his commandments.

How she had the great privilege to be affianced and later married to this one who was so different, who did not belong to the order in which she lived, we don't know, but we do know that she was married for she is recorded as being his wife.

Perhaps she had been taken to the edge of the forest where people would go to mock at this family who were toiling, day after day and year after year, putting up this great edifice that was not even on a firm foundation. It had to be shored up. She must have wondered what it was all about, and maybe had joined in the jeering and perhaps stone throwing of the people who thought that Noah and his family had surely gone mad.

She would have heard this grand old man take time from his work to stretch his back and tell them that because of his grief at their wicked ways, God was going to send a flood to wash away all that was so displeasing to him. But they had never seen rain. How could it be that water would come down from heaven? All they knew was a mist each morning that gave freshness and fertility to the land.

Maybe she had caught the eye of the young man who strove to continue with his labours in spite of the venom of the hecklers who stood around. It must have been so hard to be different from all the other boys. No hunting forays or wrestling contests for him. As soon as he was walking he had been helping his mother to carry food to his father, or assisting by passing the axe or holding the nails. Soon he was a master woodsman and carpenter himself and year after year he toiled on.

Of course Shem would have noticed this young maiden who was interested in him. He was human. He would have liked to have been building a house and settling down with her to raise their own family. What had he to offer her? Nothing in that life, only the promise that if she would throw in her lot with them that she would be saved. And we know that that was enough. She was willing to be Mrs Shem, and in choosing him she was choosing his God, and looking for a city that has foundations.

8

Now her every endeavour was joined with them in the building of the ark, in the stocking up with supplies and eventually herding the animals inside. Yes, she too would have had to endure the mocking and rejection. This was her life now, that they might be saved, and I am sure she must have pleaded with her friends and families that they too might join with them, for there was room for the whosoever.

Did they wait until the ark was almost completed before they were wed, or marrying, did they deliberately wait, knowing that they must not bring their children into such a world of violence and wickedness? Perhaps they trusted in God to do the family planning? We don't know, but we do know that it was just Noah and his wife and his three sons and their wives who entered into the ark.

They haven't bothered to tell us her name. It is a wonderful privilege to be the wife of a good man, and I am sure that she was content to be known as Shem's wife, proud to share his name. She gave up all other pleasure that she might be among the saved, and hers was the privilege, not only of enduring those long days and nights when God's judgments were let loose on a world that had forgotten him, but of stepping out into a beautiful new world and of bringing to birth a family who would help to repopulate the earth and, fearing God, would lead others to know him.

CHAPTER 2

LEADING LADY

Any woman would have been proud to have been married to Job, to be pointed out as his wife. Even if she had not been living in the days of arranged marriages, she could not have chosen a better husband. Why, he was renowned throughout the land.

Not that it was easy being his wife. Job wasn't perfect, but he was so near to it as to make it very difficult to live with him. Her home would not have been her own, for everyone came to see her husband. It was as if they were drawn by a magnet, and he would never send anyone away.

The astronomers came with their latest theories concerning the heavens; the geologists, to show him some rare jewel that they had found in the bowels of the earth. They came from distant lands to tell of flora and fauna for there was no one more knowledgeable or interested in their findings than he.

Yes, it wasn't easy being Mrs Job, for not only did the rich and famous make their way to her door, but those that were in trouble came too. They could not walk into the town without some poor woman throwing herself at her husband's feet to beg him to intercede on her behalf, or some wretched fellow who had been mauled by a lion or otherwise disabled and unable to pursue his vocation, asking for his help. Never would he turn anyone away or make them feel that their need was too trivial. He would take time and effort for each as if he or she were the only one in the world. Sometimes she could have wished that she were that one, but she knew that she should not grumble, for she had security and honour in his shadow, and riches too. There was none dressed in such raiment as she. Her beauty was renowned.

Yes, she had security. Their only anxiety was concerning their family. Of course she was lonely since the children had all left home, and they weren't happy about all this partying they heard about, but her husband used to pray for them and offer up sacrifices on their behalf, so everything must be alright.

Then came the terrible day when her world began to collapse around her. Their wealth, their family, all was snatched away from them. Strange how one messenger always managed to survive the disaster in order to bring them the terrible news, as if there were someone who wanted to make sure they were not living in a fool's paradise.

She had become an old woman overnight. She was racked with weeping, but nothing seemed to shake the faith of her husband. How could he continue to affirm that God was good? Had he no feelings?

Then it started, the attack on his body. No doubt now that he had feelings, for it was terrible to see his suffering. Now too they were proving how fickle was friendship. Where were the rich and the famous, or even the poor who had been so quick to run to him? Their halls were empty.

We feel for Mrs Job. How could she wish for her husband's life to be prolonged? There was nothing left to live for. If there had been doctors who could have administered a drug to assist him to die she would have pleaded with Job to call for them. It would have been merciful indeed. Instead she begged him to take what she was sure would be the easy way out. 'Curse God and die.'

Surely he would understand that it was out of love that she had made the suggestion; that she couldn't bear to see him suffer any more? But he answered her as if she too had become his enemy. She could not forget the reproach in his look as he spoke those never to be forgotten words, 'Shall we indeed accept good from God and shall we not accept adversity?'

If he would not help himself she must take the only course left to her, withholding her care in order that he might die the more quickly. What kindness could there be in prolonging his agony? Of course he knew that his stinking sores had made him repulsive yes, even to her. His servants whom he had treated as family and he thought had served him with devotion over the years, had left him. She did her best to convince herself that she was doing him a service.

All he had left were his comforters, 'Miserable comforters indeed,'as Job bitterly complained. We can imagine his wife listening from afar and knowing in her heart that their accusations were untrue, yet she could not bring herself to rise to his defence. Her life as a widow could not be more desolate than it was now. Death for her husband must be the only way out.

But at last Job's long trial was over. God drew near to reveal Himself to his servant. It was not at all as he had thought. He had longed that he might be able to plead his cause, to justify himself, but when he was aware of the burning brightness of holiness, of God's awesome presence, he had not a word to say. He could only bow in deep repentance. Yes, Job the upright, the benefactor, the scholar, knelt before his Maker and acknowledged himself a sinner. He hadn't had any of his questions answered, but he had found healing and wholeness. He was content in not knowing the answers, because he knew the One who did, and he could trust Him.

Whether or not Job's wife ever knew the whole story as it is so wonderfully told in the Bible we shall never know, but we do know that she must have been glad, so very glad that her husband had not listened to her when she had wished him to die. She must have been ashamed that she had not stood with him in his steadfast faith in the Lord, yet what a wonderfully happy ending there was to her story.

Assured of her husband's love and forgiveness, there was nothing of the old woman about her now. Her youth had been renewed as she felt new life within her womb and in time one child after another was brought forth. They could never replace the children she mourned, yet they filled her life with joy, a joy that was all the sweeter and fuller because of the deep valley of sorrow through which she had passed.

She wasn't stupid. She must have known that it isn't like that for everyone. For many there is no happy ending in this life. They must wait until they have passed through death to have things made right, but however great their suffering I am sure that she would have wished to tell them that life is a precious gift. She would have wanted to encourage them to cry out, as her husband had done in the depth of his despair, 'I know that my Redeemer lives,' and to tell them that, however dark the night, we must never ever, give up hope but ever turn our faces towards the sunrise.

CHAPTER 3

WOMEN ARE WITHOUT
WIFE TO THE HIGH PRIEST
The Book of Exodus

Oh yes, she had a name, but if we were to hear mention of the name Elisheba I doubt if any of us would know who she was. But we know that Aaron, the high priest had a wife because of the sons she bore.

It can't have been easy to have been the wife of the high priest of the Most High God. Of course when Elisheba was first married to Aaron he was special to her, but he would have been just one of the Hebrew people suffering under the cruel bondage of the Egyptians. She was setting up home and bringing her children into a terrible world where there seemed to be no hope, no comfort. Would her boys too grow up to labour in the brick fields of Egypt, under the lash of the cruel task masters?

But there had always been something special about Aaron and his family, for they had all believed that God had not abandoned them and that his younger brother was saved for a purpose.

Maybe Elisheba didn't know too much about Moses and how he had been delivered from a watery grave to be brought up in the palace of the Pharoah, or how, in seeking to be a deliverer, he had had to flee from the wrath of the king and live as an outcast in the wilderness.

'How can you know that he is alive, even?' she must have complained when she heard that her husband was intent on going to find him. 'And even if he is alive, what possibility is there of you meeting up with him?'

But he had met up with him. Against hope Aaron had believed in hope, and it is recorded that 'he went and met him (Moses) in the mount of God and kissed him.' Elisheba could not doubt that her husband too was someone special after that, for he became Moses' spokesman. Together they were the leaders and deliverers of their people, and a great responsibility was laid on her to be a wife worthy of the one who eventually was called to be the High Priest.

Yet she had no public position. When at last they had been delivered from the cruel yoke of slavery that the Egyptians had placed on them and came to Mount Sinai, and all the ritual connected with the Tabernacle was established, there was no ministry for women, not even the wife of the High Priest. Yes, they had been needed to bring their jewellery and mirrors, silver and gold to make all the wonderful artifacts. Perhaps she had been one who had helped to weave the curtains and even the veil which must ever exclude them from entering into the very presence of God. But there was no place for women within the holy courts. To do some menial duties outside the gate maybe, but not for them to know the Shekinah glory or to hear the voice of God.

It takes a truly great person to support another to take the lime light, to be a partner, a helpmeet, even though unrecognised or unnoticed. Elisheba would have known, more than any other, not only the strengths but also the weaknesses of her husband. Doubtless she was aware of that weakness in Aaron which caused him to fail God and his people when they thought that Moses had perished in the Mount and would not return. Maybe she herself was part of that weakness, thinking it more important that he should be in favour with the people than that he should stand on the side of the Lord.

'Don't fear the people, husband. Trust in God. Moses will come again. Stand up to them, and others will stand with you.' If only she had spoken out, daring to believe, then maybe this story, which brings such disgrace to her husband's name, might never have been written. She would not have had to squirm as she listened to Aaron making his pitiful excuse to his brother, 'I cast the gold into the fire and there came out this calf.'

There was another time when her husband was in trouble. He and Miriam had complained to Moses about his wife. Whether this was the woman he had married when he had fled to Midian, having recently returned to him, or whether he had taken another we cannot be sure, but we can imagine the jealousy that might have arisen, primarily from Miriam who, as a prophetess, would have had a close relationship with her brother. But it could well have been that Aaron's wife, instead of speaking quiet words of reassurance to quench the seeds of bitterness and dissatisfaction, added fuel to the fire.

Did she reap what she had sown when her two sons turned against their father? They too were not content with being in subjection to their leaders. It was an act of rebellion when they offered strange fire and were slain. What a bitter harvest for their mother.

We can't necessarily blame the waywardness of the children on the parents. We know that some children who have had exemplary homes have gone astray, for we are all children of Adam, and born with a bias toward sin. But we do know that wives have great influence on their partners, even if they do not share in their public ministry, as have mothers on their children.

Yes, doubtless Elisheba sometimes failed to exert the influence for good she should have done, but I'm sure that at other times she rose to her calling, for there were occasions when rebellion was again voiced against these two men of God, and in a wonderful way God vindicated her husband. Each leader had to lay his rod of authority before the Lord, but it was Aaron's alone that miraculously not only budded but brought forth fruit.

'Elisheba, it is time for me to leave you. God is calling me.' Her husband was about to die, but it does not say that his wife was among those who accompanied Aaron into the mount and who witnessed his death. It must have been hard to have been a wife in those days. Yet even though she may not have been there, doubtless she was honoured and was prominent in the days of mourning that were held by the whole nation.

Yes, it is a great honour and responsibility too to be the wife of a good man, though I am glad that through Jesus Christ we are brought into the day of grace where there is neither male nor female and we are all called to be priests and ministers in the temple of God; we dare, yes, have confidence and boldness to enter into the most holy place, within the veil, to hear the voice of God and to behold his glory.

CHAPTER 4

HOPE FOR THE HOPELESS -
MOTHER OF A HARLOT
Joshua chapters 1 - 6

There were excuses. There always are. But to have a daughter who would engage in such a profession!

As her mother, she might have known the sad circumstances that had driven her child down this slippery slope. Had the husband, protector and provider, been killed in battle; or that which is far worse, had she been deserted? We don't know the story that led to her engaging in a profession that could only destroy her, but we can imagine how the mother's heart must have ached as she heard that her daughter Rahab had fled to the city for refuge. She doubtless went, thinking its streets paved with gold. Instead she had found a city doomed. But there was no escape. She must ply her trade.

Her mother would have understood that it was those who were jealous of her beauty who gave her the title, harlot, for doubtless many of them engaged in the same profession. We may be sure that someone carried her the news.

Was she still living on the plains, or had she and her family taken refuge in the hills when the strange message came? 'You must come to my house here in the city. It is the only way that you will escape.'

Not only had they been troubled by the increasing violence of the plains people, of the sickness that was spreading through the city, but they were hearing with dread of the enemy that was approaching, the Hebrews who had crossed the desert and were threatening to invade their land. But a place of refuge in Jericho? Surely their safety was as far from there as possible. But Rahab was insistent and somehow the mother knew that they must accept this offer, even from so wayward a daughter.

So it was that her mother and father, with others of her family, found themselves crowded into this little apartment that was built into the very walls of the city of Jericho, and it was here that they found a different Rahab from the rebellious child who had left their tents so long ago. They had been directed there by asking for the Harlot's house. Oh, the disgrace. Yet her daughter stood before them now, unashamed.

'Come on then, Rahab. Tell us what has happened? Why have you brought us here? You could have got out before the city was under siege.'

She listens as her daughter begins to tell them of how she had first come to the city thinking she would find freedom, but instead was caught as a bird in a net; she tells of the misery and hopelessness of her situation; of the increasing violence and of the spreading plague. It was all so hopeless!

'Hopeless!'

As she talks, her mother must be beginning to search her own heart, to wonder how much she had been responsible for this daughter's decadence. She is sharing the feeling of hopelessness, until Rahab goes on.

'And then the rumours started, not only of the Hebrews approaching, but of their God, who fought for them. Everyone else seemed to be terrified, but I was hearing these stories of a God who was greater than the miserable, mean gods that we worship; a God who demands morality and holiness, yes, but who supplies the need of his people and who brings them through every attack, from within and without.'

Whether her daughter told them what final indignity it was that had driven her to hope in this God we don't know, but we know that the mother heard how, in that city doomed to destruction one had dared to lift her heart and believe that there might be deliverance from the shame of her present situation.

'I don't know if I even prayed in words, but somehow God must have heard, for after that everything changed. I was changed. I knew that I could no longer go on living as I was, and yet, what could I do? The men would break my door down if I were to lock it.

'When I heard footsteps on the stairs I was terrified, but as soon as these men came through the door I knew that they were different, that they were of this other kingdom.'

Her family would have heard the story of the two spies, of how Rahab had hidden them, putting the soldiers off their scent, and then helped them to escape, after they had given her their pledge that her life would be spared.

'And not just mine. All my family. Oh, how thankful I am that you listened to my message and you have come.'

The mother would remember now how hard it had been for them to trust this appeal from a daughter who had brought them shame, but now that they were there she knew that they had done right. This was a different Rahab. Only God, the God of the Hebrews, the God that the old king Melchisedek had served, in her grandparents days, could have changed her. Why, hadn't He brought them there to protect their daughter? No men could trouble her while they were all crowded with her into her tiny house.

The days of waiting must have been very hard, especially if they had been used to living out in the wide open spaces, and I am sure that some of the family would have wanted to leave their refuge. But I like to think that the mother stood by her daughter, for who more than she could know that she was truly changed, and what is more convincing than a changed life?

She wasn't Rahab the Harlot now. She was Rahab the missionary. All those in her house would be saved. Can we imagine her going through the city with God's promise of deliverance, inviting them too to come?

It is one thing to accept salvation, but the time of waiting can be hard. Even when the army finally approached, there was no sign of attack. Did her mother support her as Rahab would have had to plead with them to stay in the little house with the scarlet cord in the window?

She must have wondered how they could possibly be saved. The city could only be taken if the walls were destroyed. This must be the most dangerous place of all.

Against hope her daughter hoped, keeping her family around her. When the rams horns blasted fear into the hearts of others, to her they sounded victory, for already she was a citizen of another kingdom.

The miracle happened. While the rest of the walls crumbled, the house with the scarlet cord still stood, for the Lord knows how to preserve his own.

Because she dared to share the faith of her daughter her mother too was brought out of Jericho, out of a decadent life style, out of the kingdom of darkness.

But it is one thing to be brought out, and another to come in. It was up to her now, along with Rahab to come into the kingdom; to become part of the family of God.

It isn't easy to adapt to a different culture, as many a missionary has found.

There were so many lessons that this mother, together with Rahab and her family had to learn; new ways, new laws. Like her daughter in law, Ruth, after her, Rahab was happy to humble herself, delighting to be included in the family of God, knowing that however dishonourable her past, she was being given a new beginning. She belonged. It must have been because of her quiet confidence and joy that Salmon, a prince among his people, desired her as his wife.

Can we imagine the joy of this mother, who through her daughter's obedient faith had also been brought in? At one time she had shared her daughter's disgrace, but now she was seeing her honoured by God and his people. As she too had come to turn her face toward the sunrise she came to prove that there is always hope for our children, hope for the hopeless.

CHAPTER 5

THE WOMAN WHOSE HUSBAND WAS DISGRACED
The Book of Ruth

We don't know the name of this woman, or even of her husband, but we do know that he was publicly disgraced, and for what? It can only have been for the sake of his own wife and family.

We all love the story of Ruth the Moabitess and how, for love of her mother in law and her mother in law's God, she left her own people and land and came as a stranger among the people of Bethlehem.

She wasn't a young woman, for she must have been married to Chilion for some years, and the darker skinned Moabites would not have been attractive to the men of Bethlehem. It was not her natural beauty but rather her grace and gentleness to her mother in law that made people notice her and caused Boaz, on whose land she had gone to glean, to seek to protect and provide for her.

If it had not been for Naomi's deliberate planning, it is doubtful whether Boaz would ever have thought of marriage. We don't know what tragedy lies behind the fact that this obviously mature man was in need of a partner. There are many stories yet to be told.

Can we imagine Boaz, wearied from a hard day threshing the wheat, and then having shared a celebratory meal with the other workers, for this was not only a communal effort but a time for rejoicing, he lay down beside his own heap of grain, falling into a deep and untroubled sleep. But suddenly he is conscious that he is not alone. He stirs, and sits up, to find a woman sharing his bed. No, it is not some forward creature seeking to seduce him, but one lying in the position that a slave would take, warming his master's feet while showing that he was in need of his protection.

How his heart must have stirred as he realised that this beautiful young woman, for so she must certainly have appeared to him, was claiming her right to his protection as her kinsman redeemer.

How eagerly he must have desired to answer her request, not only to take on the responsibility of Naomi's inheritance, but to father her children through Ruth. Though they had been unaware of a growing affection there had been mutual respect as they had laboured within sight and sound of each other through the long days of harvest and now, as her need was expressed, it must have blossomed into love. With desire he desired to take her to his heart and home. But there was an obstacle.

There was another who had a greater right, who was a nearer relative.

Who was this one? Naomi had not seemed to be aware of the possibility of this one helping them. Years had passed since she had left Bethlehem and so much had happened. Maybe they had not known of the family ties, or could it be that, aware of the claim that might be made upon him, he had deliberately distanced himself from her and her need.

But if Boaz was to take on Naomi's inheritance, it had to be done legally. He had to give this other the opportunity to add this land to his. And yes, when Boaz approached him he was quite willing for this. But to take on Ruth,to father a child for her so that the line of Elimelech should be continued, was another matter. No he was not willing. He would relinquish all claim to the land.

The transaction had to be settled legally. Before the assembled elders, there by the gate of the city, which was like the court house in later times, Boaz removed the sandal of this man. The deed was done.

For us this man has no name, except 'the man whose sandal was loosed,' but he was never to be forgotten, for he had been publicly disgraced.

Surely it wasn't a big thing that was asked of him, to have another woman who would be as a concubine, living as an unpaid servant in his house. Ruth wasn't unattractive, if she had come from the heathen Moabites. She was strong and able to work for her living.

Many a man would have thought it a bargain, for it wasn't unknown or unacceptable in their culture that a man should have more than one wife.

But this man was willing to accept public disgrace for the sake of private harmony. He valued his own inheritance. He was not willing to risk hurting his own wife or to have discord or jealousy in his home for the sake of enlarging his inheritance or his name.

How grateful Boaz must have been that this man was willing to be known as 'the man who had his sandal loosed,' in order that he might claim his inheritance; not an inheritance of lands so much, as of love and of joy, for we are sure that he took Ruth to be the queen of his heart and his home. And Ruth, who once was afar off, became exalted. She belonged to the family of God and her name is recorded for ever as being a forebear of our Lord.

But there was another woman in Bethlehem whose heart was warmed. Perhaps she had been one who was insecure, never able to believe that she was truly loved. Others may have thought of it as a disgrace, but she should have been so proud, for it was for love of her that her husband had suffered shame. It was for her sake, and that of her family that he had had his sandal loosed. She was secure at last in the knowledge that she was loved, truly loved. She too could live with her face towards the sunrise.

We all need that security. That is why our Kinsman Redeemer not only offers us his protection, but was despised and rejected, suffering shame that we might have the assurance that we are loved, truly loved.

CHAPTER 6

MOTHER OF A KING
1 Samuel chapters 15 - 31

Her son was one of the greatest kings throughout the history of the nations, yet no one has even recorded her name.

We know that her husband was a great land owner, a judge and leader to his tribe. She must have been a woman of standing and influence, yet probably when her husband and sons were invited to a feast in order to meet with the prophet Samuel she would not have been invited. She had been born into a man's world.

We can imagine her organising her busy household, helping in the running of the estate, counselling her husband in all the decisions he had to make in his role as judge, besides bringing up her children. It isn't easy having a household of boys. The cuddly babies soon grow big and boisterous, and each one has his own characteristics. There is need for one to act as referee, and to bring order out of the many chaotic situations that arise and Mrs Jesse was well able to fulfil her role as peace maker. But when an eighth child was born, probably as she had thought that her time for child bearing was over, was she pleased that it was yet another boy? Did she think of the number eight as one that speaks of new beginnings, or did she, as her sons probably did, resent the intrusion he made into a life that had become more settled?

I am sure that as his mother, she often had to act as arbiter, and to take the part of her youngest against her other sons who were fast becoming young men. Was it her wisdom that had sent him away to the hills to help the servants to care for the flocks? It wasn't usually the task of a son of the household, especially in such a prosperous family, but perhaps she realised the need of her youngest to be isolated sometimes from the hurly burly of life at home, though out on the hills above Bethlehem there were other dangers. She would have watched as she saw how her son was gaining in strength and confidence as he had to battle against weather as well as wild animals that would have preyed on the flock.

Once she heard of the prophet Samuel's mission I am sure that her mother heart would have known which of her sons it was that was special. Like another mother whose Son was born in Bethlehem, she hid these things in her heart, not dreaming that it would be so long before the prophetic act would become fact and she would find herself mother to the king of Israel.

Was it she, I wonder, who, on hearing of the distressing melancholy of their present king, Saul, had suggested that the sweet music that her son produced might bring him some relief? Maybe David had often sung and played to her, restoring her to calm and confidence, and mothers have their own way of bringing their sons to the fore. Yet she must have had misgiving in her heart as she saw him go away, and how she must have longed for his visits home when they would hear all about life at court.

She must have been so thankful that her youngest was at home when war with the Philistines was declared. It was bad enough to see the three eldest go off, prepared for battle. Why her husband did not send one of the servants to see how they were getting on and to take them supplies we cannot say. Yes, she knew, she believed that one day her little David would be king, but Saul was still on the throne. This was a time yet to come. There was no danger in this mission.

It did not take long for the news to come back to them in Bethlehem, of the victory of a shepherd lad against the champion of the Philistines. Her pride would quickly have turned to apprehension, for soon, too soon, King Saul realised the threat that David posed. His heart was filled with jealousy, and the life of her son was now constantly in danger.

Sometimes those standing on the sidelines suffer more than those who are in the battle. It must have been terrible for his aged parents, not knowing where their son was, yet realising that he was being hounded, as a hunted animal, hiding in the rocks and caves. For King Saul had openly declared his hostility, naming David as an enemy of the kingdom. There was opportunity for any, like the evil Doeg, to report his whereabouts to the king, in order to receive a reward.

The parents must have known that they were being watched. They longed to see their son, and yet feared that he should come, lest he be caught in a trap. And their own lives were in danger, for in siding with their son were they not enemies of the king?

Was it at dead of night that the messengers came? 'David has a camp, up in the stronghold at Engedi. We are going to join him. Come with us. You aren't safe here.' So it is recorded that many gathered to David there in that hill fortress, and his parents came too. She who had had a fine house and servants around her, now had to face the spartan life of an army camp, and a camp that was continually on the move.

David was concerned for his parents. This was no life for them, yet he dare not send them back to Bethlehem. He had to come to a decision. He sent envoys to sound out the king of Moab, and then went himself to ask that he might leave his parents in his care.

What was life like for David's mother, there in that heathen kingdom? We know that her husband's grandmother, Ruth, had been from Moab, and doubtless this woman, strong in the Lord, accepted her exile as being an opportunity to bring their God to these people who were still in darkness. But how her heart must have yearned to hear good news of her son, to know that his long years of tribulation had ended and God's word to him had been fulfilled.

We don't hear mention of them again. Doubtless they would soon enough have heard the news of Saul's defeat and death. It was their tribe, the tribe of Judah, that was the first to acclaim David as king. Was it his aged father who, returning in haste, had gathered them together for the coronation? There were yet seven long years before the whole of Israel united to acclaim him, and his glorious reign began. Whether his mother was still alive to see her son honoured we don't know, but we may be sure that she had seen the potential in her son, and had believed that God's purposes would be fulfilled. Maybe she had had faith for a reign of peace and prosperity that could only be fulfilled in great David's greater Son, and we know that this vision is for an appointed time. Of the increase of His government and of peace there will be no end.

CHAPTER 7

THE CHILD MINDER
2 Samuel chapters 4 - 9

It is not an important job to be a nurse, a child minder. No one is going to record your name, or remember you, unless of course the unthinkable happens, and the child is injured in some way while in your care. Then it is you who are to blame. You will never be forgotten.

It can't have been an enviable task to have been nurse to the young prince, Jonathan's son, for there must have been conflict in the home, and everyone feels the effects of that.

'Jonathan! How can you side with David? You know that he will take the throne! If you don't care about your rights, what about your son? He should reign after you! But if David is made king then we will all be put to death.'

And Jonathan would seek to reassure his wife, telling her of the solemn pledge that he and David had made, that whichever of them came to power, they would show mercy and kindness to the family and offspring of the other. It was a sacred vow, a covenant that could not be broken.

Jonathan had implicit faith in the word of his friend. He knew that God's hand was on David, and that in giving him his support he was on the Lord's side. He had to believe that to side with the right would be for the ultimate good of his wife and family too. But while he did all that he could to strengthen and support his friend who had become an outlaw and a fugitive, there must have been foreboding in the heart of this one who was nanny to the little prince Mephibosheth.

Dark clouds were gathering over Israel. David, the only one who could have rallied their forces against the enemies that were threatening their land, had fled into the land of the Philistines. Jonathan stood valiantly by the side of his father, King Saul, but bravery was not enough. God had taken his blessing from Saul.

There must have been anxiety in the royal tents as they waited for news of the battle. At last a messenger limped into the camp with the terrible news. Saul is dead. Yes, Prince Jonathan too. They are sending for David to make him king.

There was panic in the royal household. Even if Jonathan's wife had believed that David would keep his promise, how could she be sure that his followers would know of his solemn pledge? Saul had hounded and persecuted David and now would be his chance to take his revenge. They were in danger, and her son most of all.

'Mephibosheth, Nanny! Take him. It doesn't matter about me, but take the young prince to safety. Run! Run for your life.'

Run she did. Can we imagine the terror, the dark; perhaps running through deep woodland, for they must keep from the main tracks? The inevitable happened. The nurse tripped and the child was thrown to the ground. No time to look for a physician to have his little legs put into splints. Holding her hand over his mouth to stifle his screams she had to continue their onward flight.

Her name is not recorded because of her valour in saving the little prince, but only because she dropped him. We are so quick to remember people's failings and not their faithfulness, but I am sure that she was faithful, caring for the child through those terrible days when nobody knew who could be trusted, who was for them and who against.

Eventually they found a haven in Lodebar, in the north, where Ishbosheth was king. He was of the family of Saul. They were safe. But gradually the people were going over to the side of David. Not only did she see this child who was so precious to her growing up as a cripple because of her, but she must constantly try to hide his identity.

When he was small she had dressed him with pride, encouraged him to hold up his head and to behave as a prince of the realm, one who would eventually sit on the throne. But now she could only advise him how to survive, to keep his head down, to remain unknown.

I hope that dear woman was still alive when Mephibosheth was eventually restored to a place of favour in the royal palace. It must have been many years later, for by this time Mephibosheth had a son of his own. I wonder if she had held the little one in her arms, rejoicing that he was not crippled as his father was.

But David had not forgotten his promise made to Jonathan. After long years, now at last the kingdom was established. He had leisure to think about his responsibility. How sad he was that Jonathan, his dearest friend, had died there on Mount Gilboa beside King Saul. He was not there to share his prosperity. But wasn't there someone left from the house of Saul so that he could keep his promise?

Mephibosheth must have been terrified when they sent for him. But how could he be in any way a threat to the king? Surely he was no better than a dead dog?

I wish she might have known, that poor woman who had to take the blame for her young master being crippled, how he was so wonderfully restored, once again treated as being of royal blood and given every respect.

If it had been today I am sure that David would have paid the best physicians to remedy his crippled condition, but he did the best he could and gave Mephibosheth a white donkey to ride on.

Dear faithful woman!

If we are given the privilege of caring for the children of others, I hope that we may find comfort in knowing that her story had a happy ending.

CHAPTER 8

MOTHER OF THE TRIBE OF DAN
2 Chronicles chapter 2

His father was a man of Tyre. King Solomon had appealed to Hiram, King of Tyre, for help in the building of the Temple. Hiram was a Phoenician, worshipper of Baal, yet because of his friendship with David, he was more than happy to acknowledge his God and now to help his son Solomon in this project. He supplied him with an abundance of timber for his building project, and grain to help with the feeding of his workmen, and also he sent him this wise and skilful master craftsman. Not only would he work on this wonderful building whose glory and magnificence was to outshine all others, but he was to train the Israelites in these special skills that he possessed. It does not give the name of this highly acclaimed person, but it does record, that though his father was from Tyre, his mother was of the tribe of Dan.

What story is hidden here? What must it have meant for this woman to have left the people of God and to have been taken away to live among a people of a different tribe, tongue, and traditions.

Of course there was a lot of infiltration, especially on the borders of their country. Doubtless they had worked out some sort of trade language. We know that early on some of the tribe of Dan, lacking faith to possess the land originally designated to them by Joshua, had moved up to the north. You may remember the sad story of how, in their travelling, they took captive a Levite, and the household gods that belonged to someone else, thinking that it would in some way bring them blessing. In settling down in the north it is likely that they had sold themselves to the Philistines, maybe having to give a portion of their labour and their produce in return for permission to live in the land. Did they also have to make payment by acknowledging their gods and bowing to them? In the book of Revelation there is not even mention of the tribe of Dan. Is this an oversight, or was there no godly remnant who had continued to put their trust in God? I believe this little story, tucked in among the Chronicles of Israel, is proof that there were still some who lived with their face toward the sunrise, their trust in the living God.

In those days a woman did not have much, if any say, as to whom she was to marry. If she were especially beautiful, or skilled in some way, then she would be considered of worth, and likely to be offered in response to some bargain. It could be, of course, that her father had some working relationship with this man from Tyre and he, seeing the daughter, had desired her and approached the father asking that she be given to him as his wife. Knowing that it was useless to object, she would have accepted her situation. I am sure there was some physical attraction, but that can never make up for the discomfort of being unequally yoked, and if she had been brought up as a godly Israelite it would have been with great pain in her heart that she prepared to raise a family.

Their good king David had been used by God to unite the tribes of Israel and to lead them in returning to their worship of the great Jehovah God. There would have been a rising faith in her heart. Now, living over the border, she would have heard news that King David's plan to build a magnificent temple was at last being implemented. The work had begun. Yes, God was blessing Israel, but meanwhile her son was in bondage to Baal and the misery that his worship brought.

It is wonderful to know that we have a God who is not bound by time and place. There is no land so dark, no people so godless, that he is not only able to protect us, but also to work out his purposes. We can never go beyond his reach, and if we have a heart to seek him there is no cry he will not hear and answer.

Can we imagine this woman suckling her little son, praying that in some way he might be a special child; praying that, in spite of the beliefs of his father and countrymen, that he might be a servant of the living God? Can we see her rejoicing as, a child now, he brings to her a little ship that he has carved, or some bird or animal? As he grows older he develops an interest in metal work. Maybe this time his offering is some carefully entwined ornament. It is obvious as he continues to develop that her child has special skills. Perhaps he had inherited them from her own father or grandfather. Such gifts cannot be hid, and would eventually have come to the attention of the king, but of what use was such talent if it were only to be used to help to adorn this alien culture?

Had this woman been praying over the years, watching her child grow, feeling there was no possibility of her prayers being answered and yet continuing to pray because the Holy Spirit was bringing this pressure upon her? How often has someone appeared on the pages of history, the right man at the right place at the right time because a godly mother has been praying for him? We shall never know, and we cannot know what difference this woman made, but we do know that King Solomon asked Hiram king of Tyre for help in his project and he sent him a wise and skilled master craftsman, and it is recorded that 'his mother was of the tribe of Dan.'

CHAPTER 9

THE VILLAGE MAIDEN
Song of Songs

She must have known that she was not unattractive, this lass from the village of Shunem; but she had no time to care for her complexion, or try to adorn her beauty. Her brothers made sure of that. She was sent to work in the vineyards, or to care for the flocks. They determined that she should be protected from any unwanted admirers.

How it was that the king became aware of her we don't know. Perhaps he and his entourage had been out hunting, and had called in to the village for water. It could be that she was sent to fill their vessels from the well, never daring to lift her eyes or think that she might be noticed. How could she have dared to think of ever having a place in the heart of her king; he who was so great and glorious?

Then the shepherd came into her life. Ah, this was a different matter. It was natural that she should meet him as she took her flocks to pasture, though how was it that it always seemed to be when she was separate from the other village girls, and that he should appear just when she needed him?

She had no thought of romance. Since her father's death she was under the protection of her brothers, and it was for them to arrange a suitable marriage for her. She was in no hurry to be tied down. But now somehow life had new meaning for her. There was a joy in her heart as she led forth her flocks. Perhaps today she would meet this one who was so strong, and yet so tender; whose voice was more musical that the brook tumbling down the hillside, or the wind blowing among the olives; whose footstep set her heart aquiver.

Sometimes she did not have sight or sound of him. She would ask, trying not to betray her heart's secret, but she could get no satisfaction. It was as if he existed only in her imagination. Yet she knew, she knew that this was reality. This was the one that her heart longed for, who spoke to her as no other had done, who had awakened her heart to feel at last the reality of life and of love.

Then, when it seemed that she could bear it no longer, he would come to her again. How wonderful it was that she who was so well protected, shielded from unwanted admirers, could be found like this, but love had made a way.

And now it was no longer just their care for the sheep or their joy in the awakening of spring time, the song of the birds of which they spoke. He had expressed his love to her and how could she help but respond?

But what would her brothers say? What if they did not approve? He assured her that he would overcome every obstacle. There was always a price to be paid to win a bride, and he would pay it, however great the cost. He would surely come and claim her as his bride.

How long must have seemed the time of waiting. There was no sight nor sound of her shepherd. When she enquired it seemed that no one knew of him. Another was tending his flocks and made out that there was no such man. How could it be? Either she could suffer torment of doubt and fear, thinking that one had come just to tease and betray her, or else she could choose to believe this one in whom she had put all her trust; believe, though no one else shared her faith, steadfastly relying on his promise.

And so she waited, the Shulamite. Did her brothers press her to be wed to another? Probably they were in on the conspiracy, but whether or not they were seeking out another who was willing to pay the bride price, we know that the heart of the Shulamite was constant, and that when at last the cry went out, 'The bridegroom cometh', her heart leapt up and she hurried to prepare herself.

But it was not as shepherd that he appeared now. Can we imagine her amazement at finding the extravagance of luxury that was to be lavished upon her, or the magnificence of her entourage? No, it was not as shepherd that her bridegroom came to claim her. He had laid aside his glory in order to win her, but now he was revealing himself as the great king himself.

Such a beautiful love story, but this is not the end, for the village maiden had to learn to take her place and yes, exert her authority amidst all the splendour of court life. It was one thing to believe herself beautiful in the eyes of her lover when they were alone on the hillsides, but quite another when she was surrounded by the most beautiful ladies of the nations. No wonder she cried, 'I am only a wild flower in Sharon, a lily in a mountain valley.'

She had to rest in her husband's appraisal of her. In his eyes she was the loveliest of them all and she had to learn to be confident in his acceptance of her. She was raised to the throne and her perspective must be of one who reigns with her beloved.

No, it was not easy for the Shulamite. It would have been easier by far to have married a farmer from her own village, but she had experienced a great love and so she must respond. She loved her Shepherd, her Sovereign, because he had first loved her, and whatever the cost she must respond to his love and give him her all.

It is a beautiful love story, this tale of the Shulamite maid who married the great king Solomon, but it is not recorded among the holy scriptures because of her alone, but because it is your story and mine. It tells of the love of the Bridegroom for his church. Ours is the throne life because we are accepted in him. For us too, the cost may be great, but how can we fail to respond to so great a love?

CHAPTER 10

JUST A CARETAKER
1 Kings chapter 14

We are not even sure if this was a woman. Maybe it was a man that God used, or even a child, but we may be sure that there was a woman somewhere in this story, for someone had influenced the little Prince Abijah.

Although the Hebrews had displeased God in wanting a human king, yet they had continued as a God fearing nation, though they were far from serving him as they should. David, though he had fallen so abysmally, had known the wonderful secret of repentance, the assurance of sins forgiven, and had continued to lead his people in true worship and praise.

The tribes of Israel were united under David and his son inherited the throne and the glory of his father's kingdom. It was Solomon who built the temple with all the splendour of its religious ceremonies. Even when he turned from the Lord and began to acknowledge the false gods that his many wives worshipped, Israel was still a God fearing nation, and it was his laws that they sought to obey.

But Solomon had been worshipping another god, Mammon, and he is a god that is never satisfied. In his greed, Solomon began to press his people for more and more taxes and service, so that when this great king died the one hope of Israel was that at last they might escape from such oppression.

We may know the story of how they came to his son, Rehoboam, asking for some relief, but the king listened to the advice of his young men. 'My little finger is stronger than my father's waist,' he told them. 'He scourged you with whips but I will scourge you with scorpions.'

It was the last straw. Israel rose up in rebellion. It was Jeroboam who led them in their revolt. Surely it was not God's will for them to suffer such oppression? Jeroboam must be a deliverer sent from God. Had he not been chosen, and even prophesied over? But gradually the priests and many of the people began to leave their own home territory and seek to be taken back under the protection of King Rehoboam, not because he was a good king, but because, while he reigned, they could still worship the true God.

Yes, Jeroboam, who had known God's call and God's protection, had failed to trust him. He had sought to make sure that the people would follow him and stay in his territory. He didn't want them travelling to Jerusalem to attend the temple worship and pay their dues, so he erected his own shrines there in Israel. It was only a symbol, the calf. Of course they were still worshipping Jehovah. But God had shown his strong displeasure when Aaron had thrown their gold into the fire 'and there came out this calf,' and now God's blessing was taken from Jeroboam.

Very soon the spirit of these false gods was taking over, and the king was leading his people from one step of decadence to another.

But they didn't all leave, those who still feared and loved God. I believe there was a godly woman, probably a godly family, working right within the precincts of the palace. We don't always have to leave when ungodliness prevails and we seem to be in a desperate situation. Sometimes God calls us to stay, to be as salt and as light. We know that she did, for in all the darkness and corruption, there was a little child who was trusting in the true God, Jehovah. Abijah was his name.

Who had taught him, this little prince? Perhaps he had followed her around, this peasant woman, as she was sweeping the floors, or preparing the meals, and she had taken time to greet him. A child soon responds when he finds love. With his parents taken up with their pagan practices the child could well have been left to his own devices. Maybe he found where our cleaning lady stayed, and would wander in and be invited to share a meal, to play with her children and to listen to the story which was a part of the family life of every godly Israelite.

How do you know this, you ask. This story is not in the Bible. No, but the next part is.

Jeroboam and his wife had not been concerned with their child while he was well, but now he was ill. They tried every physician, every deity. He was not improving. They were afraid that he might die.

'Husband! Husband! There must be someone who can help. What about this man of God you told me about? The one who tore your garment and told you that part of the kingdom would be given to you. He is a man of God. He could heal our son!'

The king was in a dilemma now. He was ashamed to let the old man know that in his extremity he was turning back to ask a favour of God. And what would his subjects think if they saw that he was reverting to the faith of Judah?

'Husband! Husband! He will die if we don't so something.'

'Very well, then, woman. But you must take him. I can't go. He would refuse me. And he mustn't know who you are. Dress as if you are a peasant woman, so that no one will know you.'

And so she goes. Wrapping up her poor sick child, she carries him in her arms and makes her way to Shiloh. No one would know who she is or where she is going.

After enquiries she finds where the prophet lives and knocks at the door, but even before she can tell the story she has been rehearsing she hears the voice of the blind man calling out to her, 'Come in. I know that you are Jeroboam's wife. Why are you pretending to be someone else? I have got bad news for you.'

The message he gave her for her husband was of God's judgement. Then instead of coming to place his hands on the poor sick child and praying for his healing her told her to take him home. 'As soon as you enter the town your son will die.'

What a terrible judgement. Why should this little child die because of the sins of his father? What must have been the grief of the caretaker and her family who had loved and cherished this little one as if he had been their own. They had tried to tell him about God, but he was just a little child, small enough to be carried all that way in his mother's arms. How could he have understood?

Perhaps they never heard the comforting words that the old prophet had added. Maybe they had to wait, as so many of us have to, to come to that realm where there is no more sorrow or tears or pain, to understand and know that God does all things well. But someone heard and recorded it.

This is what he had told her. 'Your son is the only one of your family who will be mourned and buried, because he is the only one with whom the Lord, the God of Israel, is pleased.'

'The only one with whom the Lord is pleased.' He was young, too young to die, we would say, but he was not too young to respond to what he had been told of the Living God, not too young to put his trust in him, not too young to please him, and God was honouring him by gathering him to himself at this early age.

Thank God that someone had been there in that place of darkness, someone who had reached out in love to a little child and told him of a God who is mighty to save. Men may have seen her as just a caretaker or a cleaning lady, but in God's sight she was an ambassador, sent to accomplish his mission.

CHAPTER 11

THE SLAVE MISTRESS
2 Kings chapter 5

Every wife is delighted when her husband returns home with a gift for her, flowers maybe, or a box of chocolates. If as a soldier he has been away on a campaign, then maybe she would expect some of the booty; jewellery perhaps, taken from the neck of one of his victims. But what sort of a woman is it who would be happy when he brings her a child to be her slave? Our thoughts are for the girl, snatched from a loving home and the security of her village life. Perhaps the soldiers had swept down upon them, putting their houses to the torch, killing the men and ravaging the women. What sights had this child seen that must haunt her for the rest of her days?

But this woman, and doubtless the child too, had been brought up in a culture where slavery was accepted as part of their way of life. In the Pentateuch we find laws, not forbidding slavery, but concerning treating them fairly. So the woman would have been delighted at her husband's thoughtfulness, and doubtless the child would have been relieved that nothing worse had happened than that she had been brought to work in the household of this wealthy woman.

Probably the ladies of Syria were more in the public eye than the devout women of Israel. Doubtless she was beautiful, an adornment to her husband who was not only captain of the Syrian army but a confidant of the king. Willing and obedient, the captive maid was growing up to be a personal attendant of her mistress. We can imagine her dressing her hair and helping her to don her apparel. She was certainly aware of the grief of this great lady, even though her mistress would needs have taken great pains not to let others know because of the stigma attached to her husband's distressing skin disease.

The girl was a slave. Yes, the woman may have grown fond of her, but still she was just a chattel, and she felt no compunction when she vented her frustration on her and had outbursts of temper. The nameless child could well have felt that this trouble that had come to her captors was a judgment upon them for what they had done to the people of God, but no. She had accepted her situation, believing that though what had happened to her had seemed so wrong, she was still in God's hands. If she had sulked or wept she would have remained a kitchen maid or been sent to labour in the fields, but she had faith. Knowing herself to be loved and cared for by her great Creator God, she was able to accept her lot and even take the cares of others upon herself.

We don't know what her religious experience would have been for there was much backsliding in Israel. Many had turned to false religions and the glory of King David's reign had long departed. Yet she knew of the prophet Elisha. Could it have been to their home that the widow woman had sent to borrow every jug and pitcher they could lay their hands on? She would have heard how they were each one filled to the brim from the woman's one remaining bottle of oil. Or maybe she had worked in the fields of the woman whose child, born to her in old age, was restored to life. Yes, she may well have seen first hand one or other of the wonders that God had wrought through the prophet, for she was confident that Elisha could and would heal her master.

But the prophet wouldn't just have performed miracles, though it is these that are recorded in the Bible. Doubtless he would have taught the people to return to the old paths, and keep God's righteous laws, for it is the Word that changes people. The girl must have heard and responded to his teaching, for I am sure that it was her confidence in a God who is not only holy, but good and kind, that helped her to overcome her homesickness and serve her mistress to the best of her ability. It was surely her relationship with the living God that soon brought her from being a scullery maid to wait upon the mistress of the household.

Aware now of the distress of her mistress, she would have been praying. She would have learned of the progressive illness of her husband, the great Captain Naaman. It could no longer be kept a secret. If his servants were free they would have been leaving. The captain would no longer be able to enter the presence of the king of Syria. Their situation had become desperate, and desperate needs call for desperate measures. It was not enough for her to pray in secret. She must speak out if God was going to help them.

The captive maid believed in God, and God had been revealed to her through the prophet Elisha. 'If only the master would go to the prophet in Samaria, he would heal him' she told her mistress.

Just the word of a little girl, but the word was passed from one to another and eventually it reached the master himself and was carried from there to the king. The king, anxious to have his faithful captain restored to his service, made haste to prepare the necessary gifts and entourage, and Naaman was on his way.

We can imagine the Captain's wife, the servant girl beside her, watching as the chariot clattered out of the courtyard. The sun had not yet risen, for Naaman, wrapped around in his cloak, wanted as few as possible to see his condition. He was not a sight for sore eyes. But surely, surely he would return in the full blaze of day, showing to the world that once again he was the handsome, virile man that the king had chosen to lead his army.

It is as well that they did not have satellite communication in those days; that they did not know that instead of asking for the prophet Elisha they had gone to the King of Israel, who was in such a backslidden state that he didn't even seem to be aware of the prophet and his miraculous ministry.

It is as well that they did not hear, until afterwards at least, of how nearly the captain had returned to them without being healed because he was not willing to humble himself and obey the command of the prophet who had not even come out of his house to greet him.

How thankful they would have been, when they eventually heard the story, for his faithful servants who pleaded with Naaman to humble himself and wash in the muddy river Jordan as the prophet had commanded. The story would have been told over and over again, of how he had stepped out into the flow of the river and dipped himself right down under again and again until, on the seventh time he came out and realised that his skin was clear and healthy, like the flesh of a child.

A rider gallops into the courtyard with the wonderful news. Status of mistress or servant is forgotten as they embrace. How glad, how very glad the child must have been that she had found courage to speak out her faith.

Was the slave girl sent back to her own people as a reward, or did she find that she was at home now with these people who, having placed their trust too in the living God, had become as family to her? She may have been accounted as a chattel of one who was used to being a slave mistress, but there was surely a difference in their relationship now and because this child had been willing to speak of her faith in God we may be sure that this great lady too had turned her heart and she too was living towards the sunrise.

CHAPTER 12

THE KING'S DAUGHTERS
Jermiah 38 and 41:10

Who were they, these king's daughters, who survived the destruction of Jerusalem?

We think it must have been wonderful to have been born in a palace, to know that your father is the king, but it was not so for these little girls.

You see, their father was Zedekiah, vassal king to Nebuchadnezzar, king of Babylon. He was only twenty one when he came to the throne, and thirty one when his kingdom collapsed around him and he was carried away captive.

His wife must have worked hard to console the young man while all this political intrigue was going on around him, for it is recorded that he had sons and daughters, so there were at least four children.

The Chaldeans were renowned for their cruelty, and the brothers of the princesses met a terrible end. They were used to punish the foolishness of their father. When at last the Babylonians broke through their siege, King Zedekiah was taken before their general. Jerusalem had already been defeated by the Chaldeans, but instead of razing it to the ground Nebuchadnezzar showed his greatness by placing this young man on the throne, entrusting him to rule over the remnant who had been left there.

Now Zedekiah was made to answer for his stewardship. Instead of being faithful to Babylon, who had shown them mercy, he turned to Egypt to aid them in a rebellion. What greater punishment could they inflict on him than to see his two young sons killed, for it was the last sight he ever saw. They then blinded the young man. Dragged away in chains, the cries of his sons would have been ringing in his ears, while he would have seen over and over their last moments of anguish. How terribly he was made to suffer for his foolishness. But what of his daughters? Their fate could have been even worse.

The Chaldeans were a cruel, proud people, not renowned for compassion, and yet it seems that there was some compassion shown to those who had survived the long years of siege and famine. Gedaliah, a God fearing Jew, was made governor, and a remnant of those who had survived were left in his care. Among them was Jeremiah, and also mention is made of the king's daughters.

How had this miracle come about, that their lives had been spared? I believe it was all because of the prophet Jeremiah.

Over long years Jeremiah had warned the king and the people that the invasion of the Babylonians was God's way of punishing them, and that if they would surrender to the invaders then their lives would be saved and God would bless and eventually restore them.

Those in authority felt that by preaching this message Jeremiah was undermining their morale and preaching treason. His life was threatened, and at one time he was thrown into a cistern where he was left to sink and die in the mire.

This cistern was within the precincts of the palace. The Bible records that one, Ebedmelech, an Ethiopian, pleaded to the king on behalf of the prophet, but I like to think that it was the distress of the little girls that first moved his heart.

Brought up in the palace, they must have seen this man of God coming to visit their father. Little children are often far more aware of what is going on than we may think. Jeremiah would have seemed an austere man. He had forsaken marriage and the joy of family life because of the severity of his message, yet I am sure that somehow the little princesses were conscious of a kindness and compassion of which others were not aware.

Can we imagine them making sure that if there was bread for them to eat, that the prophet, their father's prisoner, should have some too? Had they peeped over the edge of the well, horrified that this man of God was left in such awful condition to die? Was it their anguish that had given Ebedmelech courage to go to the king and receive permission to rescue him?

Jeremiah, lifted out of this hell hole, made a promise to the brave Ethiopian that his life would be given to him as a prize. Could it be that the little girls were included in the same promise?

God's word had come to pass. The city, once so beautiful and prosperous, was razed to the ground. All who might be of any worth had been taken away in chains to serve their conqueror in far away Babylon.

'Will you come with us?' they asked Jeremiah. Because they knew that the prophet had counselled his people to accept Babylon's domination he was treated now with respect.

'No, I will stay,' was his reply. He knew that though God had allowed such punishment to come upon his land, that he had not finished with Judah; that Jerusalem would be rebuilt and prosper again. Thus he was left in the care of the godly Gedaliah, he and the king's daughters.

Surely now their troubles were over. If they did have to live as peasants, eking their living from the land that had not been burned and flattened by the armies, at least they were safe from any more warfare. Jeremiah must have thought that in choosing to stay he could live out his days in peace, caring for the young princesses as they grew up.

But there was yet more suffering for the old man and the young maidens. Gedaliah was murdered by some upstart. Another arose to deal with the murderer, but now, fearing reprisals from their overlords, they decided to flee into Egypt.

'No, don't go to Egypt. You will be safe if you stay here,' Jeremiah warned them, but in spite of all their suffering and the judgments that God had heaped upon them they still would not listen to what God was telling them through his prophet. Jeremiah, and doubtless the king's daughters, were taken against their will, into Egypt.

What happened to the beautiful young women? We know that the prophet, an old man now, was still available to his Lord, and was busy recording the words that God was giving him for the nations around. His was still a ministry of doom and gloom, and yet it was Jeremiah who was used to foretell the message of hope of a new covenant, and of God giving his people a new heart and a new spirit. Could it be that the king's daughters too shared his hope, and even in a godless country and among a rebellious people, lived out their days with their faces towards the sunrise?

CHAPTER 13

DAUGHTER OF BETHLEHEM
Matthew's Gospel

We always have the children coming to the manger. No nativity scene seems complete without the little ones, and surely the children of Bethlehem would have been there.

They would have been full of excitement as it was, with the town full of visitors, and their own houses crowded out. It wouldn't have taken much to waken to them.

Can we imagine a child listening to the whispers. - The shepherds told us. - Yes! Angels! - That was the sign - yes, that he would be lying in a manger. - Can you imagine? A baby in a manger? - But it's true! Go and look if you don't believe me.

While the adults were discussing the possibility or impossibility, the theological implications, the children would have crept in awe to where the cattle were sheltering beside the inn. There, in a quiet corner, away from all the melee of the soldiers, and many travellers, they found a young mother and her new born son, wrapped in strips of cloth, and lying in the manger where the cattle usually fed.

Was it Joseph who told them the wonderful story, of how the angel had come to Mary, telling her that this child was the Son of God; of how God had spoken to him through a dream so that he knew that he must care for this very very special child who was Emmanuel, God with us?

The children would already have heard stories of the promised Messiah. They knew that a deliver was to come who would save them from the tyranny of the Romans, but they had never ever thought that he would come in this way, as a babe, weak and helpless, as they themselves were.

The town would have been buzzing with the news, and as is always the way, some believed and others doubted, but I am sure that the children would have been sure, so very sure, that this baby was special. He was God's gift to them. Everything would be alright now because he was to bring peace on earth. Wasn't that what the angel had said?

It is easy for children to believe, and to respond to the Lord, but their faith too must be tested, and many return to him only after many years of hard trial when he has seemed to be far away. It was surely so for this little girl, one of the children who grew up in Bethlehem. How great had been her joy as she crept there to kneel at the manger. Perhaps she had run home begging her mother that she might take a jug of milk or even to make some cakes with her own little hands to carry to Mary as her way of bringing a gift to the baby.

Probably her mother realised that there was a far greater gift they could offer, and that someone must needs open not only their heart but their home to this needy family. 'No room,' they had said, but now they must make room, and for a while, a very little while, they had the great privilege of caring for the Son of God.

But her joy was short lived, her faith shattered and broken. How long it was after the birth of the Wonderful Child we will leave the theologians to dispute. We know that it was soon, all too soon, that the wise men came to Jerusalem seeking him who was born King of the Jews.

Whether they found the young child in Bethlehem, or whether the star had guided them back to Nazareth where the family had returned after their visit to the temple as Luke records we cannot be sure. It makes no difference, for there is no doubt that the soldiers came to Bethlehem.

No, they had not come for her, but this did not minimise her terror. For years to come she would awaken screaming as she relived the horror of those dreadful hours when the soldiers burst into their houses, searching into every possible hiding place to find the young children, and plunging their swords into those supple young bodies. She would hear again her mother's screams as they dragged her away from where she had thrown herself, covering her child who was so dear, so precious.

So this child who had knelt at the manger would have grown up, not only trying to come to terms with her own grief, but coping with a mother who had been traumatised. Not yet in her teens, she

48

had to be mother now, caring for this one who, still strong in body, in mind was so feeble; and she would not even wish to bring her back to reality, for life was cruel and bleak.

What of her hope now, of the Wonderful Child who was to bring peace and goodwill? Could she dare to believe that he might have survived? Even if he had not been in Bethlehem, the soldiers had gone into all the region round about. Every boy child under two years of age had been killed. Yes, the child they had thought was God's own Son must be dead, and her faith too was dead. How could there be a God when such things happened?

So she grew up, this daughter of Bethlehem, as many others must have done, and still do today. How great was her pain, how great her burden.

She would have been a mother herself, a grandmother even, and the one who should have been her strength and support still a constant drag upon her, when they began to hear talk of a prophet from Nazareth. I don't suppose any of them linked him with the precious child that they had seen, and yet, when the stories persisted, of his words of hope and many miracles of love and kindness, was there a stirring of hope, a remembering?

We don't read of the Saviour ever again visiting Bethlehem, but then Jerusalem was not so many miles away. Could it have been that this care worn daughter of Bethlehem met this Wonderful One again? And looking into his face knew that though there was so much that she couldn't understand, God was good and all was well. Did she take her poor traumatised mother, who had lost her own son because of God's Son, and ask him to lay his hands on her head and heal her?

Maybe it was not until after that first Good Friday, that darkest day in all of creation, that they found healing. She had to understand that God was willing for his own Son to undergo man's worst that we might find healing, before she could come to him again in faith. No manger now, no swaddling clothes. She was kneeling before one who has been highly exalted. He had not yet brought peace and goodwill, except in her own heart, but she knew, as we may know, that He is Emmanuel, God with us, and all is well. She could live now with her face toward the sunrise.

CHAPTER 14

THE BRIDE
John chapter 2

Though she was the most blessed of all mothers, Mary had never had her own wedding feast. Perhaps this was one reason why she was so concerned that this day, or probably week, should be very special for the young bride.

We know that girls in the Middle East were generally very young when they were married. To be the centre of so much attention, and especially over so long a period might have been an ordeal for one only just out of childhood. But probably not so, for she had been born for this. The whole purpose of womanhood in their culture was to be married and of course to bear children, and for the Jewish maiden there was always the precious hope that to her might be born the child whose name was Wonderful, the deliver of her people.

Yes, since her birth, this unnamed Jewish maiden had been preparing for her wedding day. Every task she learned around the house, every rule and regulation had been to the end that she might be a virtuous wife and mother.

There would have been only anticipation when her parents began to negotiate a suitable marriage partner for her, and it would have been with joyful acquiescence that she was called in to meet the bridegroom. Gladly she took the cup that was offered her, as together the young couple pledged their troth. She was as good as married. There was no turning back now. She belonged to this one her parents had lovingly chosen for her, but they were not yet living together. Her bridegroom was going away to prepare their home and he had given her his promise, I will come again and receive you to myself.

From then on she had lived for the day when she would hear the cry, Behold, the bridegroom is coming! She was preparing her wedding dress, as well as other more serviceable garments. She chose her bridesmaids, and they were all living in expectation of the great day of her wedding. The only problem is that none of them knows when the bridegroom will come. Months pass. There must have been some news of the progress of the house he was building, for it was a close knit community. A year passes, so they know that it must be soon. Her attendants sleep in the house now, for he might come at night. I am sure they all had had oil in their lamps for none had been shut out. There is only joy as the guests begin to arrive.

Were they especially rich that they had six large water pots supplied to wash the guests hands and feet when they entered? There were not many with houses large enough to accommodate a crowd in the little town of Cana. It is more likely that they would have set up awnings in the open air, while servants from homes around had come with the water pots, filling them for them.

There she was, in all her finery, so proud and thankful to see so many come to enjoy their celebration, bringing gifts and wishing God's blessing on their union. It would have been easier to be wearing the simple garment of a servant than the ornate robes of the bride, but she was honouring her husband and this was her hour of glory. There was an abundance of food prepared, and the wine was flowing freely.

She would have been proud that Mary's eldest son, the young teacher from Galilee had come to add his blessing, though maybe the young men who were his followers would have put some burden upon the household.

The supply of food and wine would not have been her concern. This was the one occasion in her life when she sat to be served. From henceforth she would be the one to carry all the responsibility of serving others, but no, it was not her concern, and yet a woman feels these things and she could well have been aware that there was some anxiety among those who served, as was Mary, the mother of this young carpenter who had left his trade and was just beginning his ministry as a preacher, already gathering a following.

Maybe even the bride did not know until afterwards just how wonderful was the miracle that was performed, in order that their wedding feast might not be spoiled, and that they might know that God's blessing was assured on their life together.

She would have heard, as you and I have done, of how Mary had realised that the wine was running low. Knowing that this would have brought disgrace on the young couple and spoiled the festivities, she had gone to tell her son Jesus. She would have heard how he had seemed to rebuke his mother. Why should she tell him about it? He hadn't come just as a wonder worker.

She would have learned too of the servants' dismay when he had asked them to fill again the great stone jars. They had been up early, before the heat of the sun, trudging time and again out of the town to the well in order to see that there was an ample supply. But surely they had enough to do now, and why was there a need of water?

She would have heard how all their weariness was turned to wonder as they had poured out from the jars and found that the water was turned to sparkling wine.

We don't read of the moment when the wine was passed to the bridegroom and he in turn offered the cup to his bride, but we can imagine how her eyes must have brightened. Her weariness was gone. There was a joy upspringing in her heart that she had never known before. All her doubts and fears were banished. Life was wonderful.

I don't suppose she ever again drank wine that was as sparkling or effervescent as that they shared at their wedding that day in Cana of Galilee, but it wasn't just the wine that brought her joy, but the knowledge of the one who gave it. She had caught a glimpse of the glory of God in the face of this Jesus who had graced their wedding feast.

She was soon enough just one of the women who tilled their fields, ground their corn and came morning by morning to the well. She would bare children and know the joys and sorrows of motherhood as she brought them up in an oppressed nation, but she would never forget what she learned on her wedding day, that the great Jehovah God, whom they had worshipped afar, cared for such little people as they were. He understood their worries and their cares and was near at hand, willing to intervene.

She had learned that this Creator God, who first planted the vine in the garden in Eden and gave us skill to produce wine from its fruit, is willing sometimes to speed up the miracles of nature to meet the need of men and women, not just to satisfy us or to help us in our extremities, but that others might have a glimpse of his glory and that they too might know that he is good and live with their faces towards the sunrise.

CHAPTER 15

THE MOTHER IN LAW
Matthew chapter 8

What a wonderful joy to be a grandmother, even if it invariably means hard work, but to be a mother in law - that can often be an unenviable position. We have all heard many a 'mother in law' joke, but it was no laughing matter to be left a widow in those days and have to use your claim as mother in law in order to live.

'Pure and genuine religion is this,' writes James, 'to take care of orphans and widows in their suffering.' Yes, there is suffering in being widowed, however affluent our society, but how much greater is that suffering when your means of livelihood is gone and you are dependent on the benevolence of others.

We may presume that it was being widowed that brought this woman to her daughter's house. Of course it is never easy for two women to share a kitchen, however well they get on, but then, if the women get on too well the husband may feel neglected and that can bring other conflicts.

Sharing a kitchen wasn't a problem for this mother and daughter. Most of the cooking would have been in the open air. It took two to grind the corn and there was always need of another pair of hands in those days when there were no automatic dish washers or washing machines. I'm sure that this woman, named only as Peter's wife's mother, was glad that she still had health and strength to be useful, but it was a different situation from when she had ruled in her own household.

When her son in law left his family to follow the Carpenter from Nazareth she would have had no doubt that she was needed. Maybe she even felt that it was providence that had brought her to this home. She saw the anxiety of her daughter as she cared for the little ones, dependent now on the gifts of the other fishermen, anxious that the children should not get into bad company or even into danger as they played on the sea shore in their fishing community there by the Sea of Galilee.

Yes, she was glad enough to help, but she must have wondered what sort of husband it was to whom they had given their daughter, for they had done their best to arrange a suitable marriage for her. What responsible person would leave his family to follow some itinerant preacher? Yes, he would turn up from time to time and bring his share of the gifts and money that they received, but they never knew when he was coming.

Her daughter didn't complain. It seemed that she too had listened to the Teacher, and she felt that she was doing her part in being willing for her husband to follow Jesus. But how could it be right? It was acceptable for James and John and the others. They were young men. They didn't have family responsibilities, but to take away the wage earner from a young family! Sometimes it must have seemed as bad as if her daughter had been left a widow too.

It is so easy for resentment to creep in and make its nest in our hearts. At first she would try to push away these niggling doubts, but after a few battles maybe it became easier to harbour and even to feed them. We can't blame her illness onto this of course, though who knows how much our wrong thinking is to blame for the sicknesses that come upon us? We do know that bitterness and grief may weaken us in our ability to wage war against the illnesses that constantly assail us.

I doubt if they called them viral infections in those days. We don't know whether she went down with the illness suddenly or whether for some days she had felt her strength draining from her, her head burning and her limbs aching, but we do know that when the message came that not only Peter, but the rest of the party, would be calling in, that the one who was needed most was unable to rise from her bed. She was burning with fever.

It is often the case that not until someone is missing do we realise how much we have depended on them. Maybe her own daughter had sometimes wished for the good old days when her mother had her own home, but we may be sure that now she was longing for her wise words, calming her, directing her as to which task should take priority, tending the oven while she ran to send the children about their various tasks, and in all her busyness of preparing a meal she was concerned for her mother. She should have been with her, holding her hand, listening to her dying requests.

It was into the hurry, scurry and worry that Jesus came. It may have been one of the little ones who took the Master by the hand and brought him into the darkened room to where their dear grandmother lay, tossing and turning. Can we imagine her opening her eyes, conscious that someone has entered the room, seeing beyond the little one to look into the face of the one who had taken away her son in law, the one whom in her heart she had been accusing. She looks now and sees his hand reached out to her, taking her work worn hand in his, and looking into her eyes. This is not just some wandering preacher. This is the one who has made her, who knows her inmost thoughts, her deepest needs. Perhaps she does not understand this, but she does know that he understands not just the pain of the fever but the distress of her widowed state, her resentment concerning the way her daughter was treated. He understands, yes, and he is taking away all the pain.

Looking into his eyes she knows that he not only understands but he forgives. As he grips her hand she feels fresh strength surging through her being. The Master doesn't stay. There are other needs to attend to and in any case, there is no need. Mother in law is healed. There she is, once against attending to her many household duties, speaking a word of direction to the children, taking the weight from her daughter's task, serving the Saviour.

Yes, she had the great honour of serving Jesus, not only in his brief visit to that fisherman's dwelling there in Capernaum on the shores of Galilee, but for the rest of her life. She knew that whatever burden was pressed upon her, she was serving the Master, and each duty became a delight. Maybe she still did not understand why it was that the father of the household had to leave them, but she had looked into the face of the one who had reached out and touched her in her distress and knew that she could trust him even where she could not trace. I am sure that Peter's wife's mother became a living example of all that God intends a mother in law to be.

CHAPTER 16

ALL THAT SHE HAD
Mark chapter 12

It must have been terrible to be left a widow in those days, dependent on the generosity of others. If she had had no children to continue her husband's line then she might have been taken by another, but her little ones meant more mouths to feed.

When her husband had moved to the city I am sure that they had looked forward to a life of prosperity. There was far more opportunity to build up his business there than in the village, and they were living under the shadow of the temple. Surely here God's blessing would be upon them.

They may have taken their firstborn there to dedicate him to the Lord. Only able to make a poor man's offering, a pair of pigeons, even so they had felt blessed. It was here that their son would be received into manhood.

She had known that it had happened to others. Why, everyone was expected to give towards the maintenance of widows and orphans, but she had never thought that it could happen to her. Was it an accident that took her husband, her bread winner from her, or just one of the wasting sicknesses that were so prevalent in that overcrowded city? Whatever it was, she must have felt that it was an evidence of God's displeasure; that she was a woman accursed.

We shall never hear the story of how she had made the journey back to her people, or of the pain of being made to feel that though they were feeding her, that she and her little ones were an unwanted burden. Sadly she had crept away without a farewell, and made her way back to the city. Turning her back on the temptation to make money the easy way, she tried to do a little trading, but her profits could scarcely stay their hunger. Her children were weak and sickly, and her own strength was failing. She must have help.

She would go to the temple. There was a fund for those who were in need. Why, the rich merchants and the religious leaders used to make a great show of taking their offerings to the treasury. Perhaps she could pluck up courage to ask, though surely if they saw her they would realise her plight.

The treasury was in the court of the women. There was a limit to how far they were allowed to go in this magnificent temple, but they made sure that the women were not excluded from giving. They could receive teaching too. The rabbis used to sit in this court, and before her first child had been born it could well be that she had come sometimes to stand respectfully to hear what they had to say.

She was not thinking of being taught on this occasion. There were more urgent matters to be attended to, or so she had thought, until she heard the voice of the Teacher from Galilee. She was arrested. For a few moments she stood and forgot her cares as she listened to the words that flowed from his lips. They seemed to bring healing. No longer did she feel despised, rejected, a burden on society, a woman accursed. He spoke of a Heavenly Father who cares for the odd sparrow, and who numbers even the hairs of our head. He spoke of the Kingdom of Heaven, that it is for those who are counted as poor in men's sight, but are rich in faith. He spoke of a Father who will never turn a deaf ear to his children but who will always hear their cry. He spoke of serving and ministering, of not being great in the eyes of men, but of the joy of giving to a God who gives his all to us.

She had come hoping to receive something, and receive she had, though not of this world's goods. If she had got around to asking, it is likely that she would only have been given grudgingly, but somehow her perspective on life had changed. Her whole being was rising up in response to the love that she felt was being poured out on her. She had come to ask, but now she wanted to give.

The Teacher had finished his sermon for that time and was sitting now over against the offering boxes, as though he was interested in seeing who should come to make their sacrifice. The receptacles were shaped like trumpets, and some were able to make a great show as they poured in their bags of coins. How dare she stand in the line with these men of wealth and fame? And what did she have to give? She only had two tiny coins, enough to have bought just a small cake for the children.

Somehow she wanted to give herself, to show her response to the great and holy God, who loved and cared, even for her. Ashamed for men to see, and yet coming because she knew that there was a greater one to please, she joined in the line with the dignitaries of the city.

Her coins were so tiny that the chink that they made could not even be heard. She must return now to where she had left her little ones. What had she done? She had nothing left to even buy them a mouthful. Her eyes filled with tears and she was about to hurry away when someone stopped her and pointed for her to listen to what Jesus was saying. Everyone was hushed, for the Saviour was speaking loud and clear, words that have been repeated throughout the ages, 'This woman has given more than you all.'

What is the end of the story? There is no record in the Gospels, but we know that in some way our faithful God supplied the needs of this poor widow woman. Perhaps Jesus himself sent his disciples to seek her out, for we know that, living by faith as they did, they were not unmindful of the needs of the poor. Perhaps like Ruth of old, the Lord provided one who would be to her a kinsman redeemer. We cannot be sure, but we can be sure that like her we can give and know that God will in some way give back to us in abundant measure.

CHAPTER 17
THE DEVIL'S MOTHER
Mark chapter 5

We don't know if he had a wife and children, but we do know that he must have had a mother, this man who was an outcast, chained up and living among the tombs. What could it have been like to have been known to have given birth to such a son? There must have been a time when she had thrilled to feel the new life within her, to have known deep comfort and satisfaction as her newborn had suckled to her breast.

Of course, we don't know what it was that had caused this one to open his heart to the enemy and his legions. Had there been some violent assault on his mother that had affected an innocent child? We know that he was brought up in Gadara, one of the ten towns of the Decapolis, with a strongly Gentile influence. That was why there were herds of pigs in that region. The Jews were forbidden to eat pork. 'Swines flesh' they called it, and pigs should have had no part in their economy. Isaiah equates the eating of swine with spiritism. Was there some link then with his upbringing that this young man was in such a desperate state?

Whether the parents were in any way to blame, or whether as a youth he had deliberately turned away from the ways of the Lord and opened his heart to the enemy we can never know, but we can be sure of the pain that his mother must have endured, and the disgrace too, so that at times she must have felt that she had given birth to the devil himself.

Maybe from the beginning he was a difficult child. She had to struggle with his screaming and his tantrums as a toddler, but as he grew stronger she had to shout for the men to come and help her to hold him. At last the parents would have had to accept that he was uncontrollable and bow to the decision of the elders of the town. This child she had carried in her womb was now bound with chains.

With what shame and grief she would have crept out to where he was, taking him food and seeking to minister to him but, though because she was his mother she could not help but love him, hatred was flashing from his eyes. She was endangering her life by going near him. Then came the cry, 'He is gone! The demoniac is gone! He has broken his chains!'

From now on she lived in the terror of his return. Would he creep up on her in the night, murdering her in her bed? It was not just the mother - the whole town must have felt as if they were in a state of siege. What would they do if he leaped upon them? There was no man who had the strength to fight him. If they hid up on the hill side and pelted him with stones, it might only drive him to a frenzy and he could rush in and wreck the town.

'He's coming.' How his mother must have dreaded hearing those words. There was no peace for her. She tried to busy herself with her daily tasks. Doubtless she had had other children who had been a joy to her, and now she busied herself in helping them in their homes, bringing up the grandchildren. There were so many beautiful things in the world, but the dark shadow of fear, yes, and of shame, takes the colour out of them all. She was as an old woman, her hair white before its time, her limbs feeble. The very thought of what he might do if he returned robbed her of her strength. Was it some sin of hers that had brought such a curse upon her life? Did God have no compassion that he should allow her to suffer in such a way?

'He's coming!' 'He's coming!' They try to keep it from her, but she is among the first to hear the news. Women are calling their children, barricading themselves inside their houses; the young men, already trained, dispatched to set a guard on the hillside overlooking the approach road. His mother does not bother to take cover. She knows that if he has decided to attack her that there is no escape, no door will keep him from her. She would only be endangering her family by hiding in one of their homes. She remembers how his wrath was turned against her, even as a child. Weeping, she makes her way to the well, just outside the walls of the town. Maybe, just maybe, he will be content to attack her and, his venom spent, will return back to the wilderness where he has been living among the rocks and caves.

She waits, but she does not hear the screams and curses that she had expected. For once in her life she seems to be aware of the kiss of the sun, the song of the birds. A man is walking along the road towards her, a tall, handsome young man of whom any mother could be proud, while the other men who had been sent out to protect them are following, wondering, behind him.

'Son? Son?' She is afraid to believe what she is seeing. It is her son, this boy who had caused her nothing but grief. He is walking towards her, not naked and filthy as he used to be, but clothed, his hair combed. Where could he have got such a fine coat? His eyes light up in recognition. His arms are open. 'Mother!' he calls. She feels the weight of her years of sorrow rolling from her as he takes her in his arms.

How proud she is to sit beside him as the towns folk gather and he tells the wonderful story of how the Master had come in his boat across the sea. The demons who were living in him had known who it was. Jesus, they had called out his name. And Jesus had seen the deep longing of his heart that he might be free from their domination and torment and had commanded them to depart.

Perhaps he does not tell them the part about them begging to enter into the pigs. There would be others who would come to tell the sad story. Many there were who had put prosperity and money before the commands of God. Their livelihood depended on their pigs. Already they were calling the town council together. The decision was made. This Jesus must go.

We don't know the rest of the story. Did the young man ever have the opportunity to take his mother and others in his family to meet this wonderful Saviour who had come to that lonely place because of his compassion, not only for his torment, but for this mother and family too? How sad he must have felt that, knowing what devastation their disobedience had brought to them, his towns folk still chose Mammon before God. But for his mother, I am sure that the rest of her days were lived with her face turned towards the sunrise.

CHAPTER 18

ADULTERESS
John chapter 8

This was no ordinary street woman. It was not a life of profligacy that they were wanting the Saviour to judge. No, it was a respectable married woman whom they had deliberately lured into sin, trapped so that her indiscretion might be avowed. She was caught, 'in the very act.'

Such things do not happen in a moment. A wife, especially one living in those times, would not easily compromise herself, risking not only her livelihood but her very life to satisfy her passion. Can we imagine the shame of this young woman, dragged into the temple courts? This was a place where they were meant to experience holy joy in knowing that there was atonement for sin, but she was brought there to be judged. It was not the blood of bulls and goats, but her blood for which they were crying, for stones to be thrown until, bleeding and torn, she yielded her last breath.

So how had it come about? Still with the bloom of youth, she was a respectable married woman who had been lured into a trap. Yes, it must have been a deliberate trap that had been set, for how else could it be that these men who were supposed to be so godly could tell the master, 'She was caught, in the very act.' Without doubt, she had been set up.

What of the one who had sinned against her, and against her husband? We don't hear anything of him. He would have been paid handsomely and sent on his way. After all, someone had to help the priests to discredit Jesus and rid them of his power and influence over the people. Yes, it was Jesus they were trying to trap. This poor woman was just a pawn in their game, expendable.

They must have known of her need. Her husband, having paid a good bride price, gave her clothing, a home and respectability, but if he did not fulfil his obligation as a husband then she was poor indeed. Doubtless knowing either of his impotency or his infidelity these schemers had realised that this young woman was vulnerable and likely to yield to temptation.

How did it begin?   He would have had to take his time, this likeable but unstable young man whom they were using. Maybe it began with a chance encounter in the market, an apparently unconscious brushing of finger tips that awakened desire. Gradually she would become aware that their meetings were not by chance, that she was attractive to him, that he was deliberately seeking her out. Starved of the affection she needed, she could not resist his attention. She began to yield to petty deception and subterfuge in order to see him until it was inevitable that when he suggested that they meet in privacy that she had no resistance left to refuse.

Perhaps others had been part of the plot, so that her husband was away, or maybe they met by day in some other house. Wherever it was, we may be sure that it was well watched, and that these 'holy' men had their entertainment.

Fearful, knowing that she was doing wrong, and yet led on until she abandoned herself to his embrace, she did not have the chance to rest in sweet contentment. It was from 'the very act' that she was dragged in shame and great fear into the temple courts, and it was there, when she felt that she could sink no further, that she saw the Master, and realised that he was looking at her, not with contempt, but with compassion. She was not afraid for him to look for she knew that he saw all that she had suffered in her love-less marriage, all the allurements that had been offered until at last she had yielded to temptation and done the unforgivable.

She hid her eyes, for even though he understood, she knew he would never condone sin. Yet even as she sought to gather her robe to cover her nakedness, she was aware of a peace surrounding the Master, so that even these beasts who had dragged her there were tamed.

'Moses commanded that such a woman should be stoned to death. What do you say?' they had asked him. At last the woman too looked up, for the silence was deafening. Jesus was bent over, writing with his finger on the ground.

Probably it was not more than a few moments, though it had seemed like hours to her, until Jesus lifted his head. 'Alright,' he told them. 'Stone her. Throw rocks at her until her last drop of blood is shed and she is dead.' A gleam came into their eyes as they began to prepare themselves for the dastardly murder. They were willing to do it, for they knew that Jesus would be blamed, but Jesus was continuing. 'The one of you who has never sinned is to throw the first stone.'

The woman stood there, encircled by these her accusers. Was she aware that Jesus was calling their bluff? They had known that they could not put someone to death with out the consent of the Romans. They were not so concerned about the woman being punished as their putting Jesus in an impossible situation. If he said she should not be put to death then he was denying the law of Moses, but if otherwise then he could be in trouble with Rome.

She was too ashamed of her own sin to be watching these men who were thought to be so righteous, so respectable. They had never thought that their indiscretions might have been brought to light, but the Teacher was writing again. Suppose he was naming him? Each one feared, not daring to cast a stone lest his hidden deeds be blazoned abroad.

She would not have known what the Saviour had been writing in the dust. She had not seen them slip out, one by one. She only knew that a strange silence had fallen over the courtyard until, looking up at last, she realised that she stood alone with the Saviour.

At last he looked up. Gently he asked her, 'Where are they? Is there no one left to condemn you?'

'No one, Lord.'

'Neither do I condemn you.' Oh, what wonderful words. He had understood her circumstances, her long years of deprivation and humiliation; the pressure of the temptation that she had tried so hard to resist, the pleasure of yielding, though that pleasure had been so short lived. Oh, how wonderful to know that he did not condemn her. But not to condemn did not mean that he condoned her act as an indiscretion. His next words made that plain.

'Go, and sin no more.'

Sin is sin, whatever the extenuating circumstances. There was no way that he would condone her leaving her husband and running off with this one who had appeared to offer her all of which she was in need.

But how could she return to her husband? Would he have her back? Surely the Master was asking more than could be demanded of flesh and blood. But she had looked into his eyes, knew that all her guilt and shame was forgiven. She did not know that he was going to take her shame, her nakedness, and bear it in his own body when he would go to the cross; that God would make an open display of how abhorrent sin is to him that we might never excuse our acts as mere indiscretions. No, she didn't know, but she had looked into the eyes of the Holy One and knew that not only did he offer her forgiveness, but power to live as he would have her.

The day would come when she would know the Holy Spirit, the Comforter, filling her with holy joy, but even now she knew that his love would sustain her.

We don't know the end of the story. We can be sure that none of those Pharisees who had gone to such trouble to catch her would have told the story to her husband. Perhaps he was an invalid, incapable of knowing what his young wife was suffering. No, we don't know, but we do know that sometimes the Saviour asks us to return to seemingly impossible situations and it is in these situations that we find him to be our refuge, our fortress, our glory and the lifter of our heads.

Some manuscripts do not include this story of the woman taken in adultery, and some would feel that I should not include it in this collection of women who turned their faces towards the sunrise, but I am so glad that it is in my Bible, and that I have a Saviour who forgives my sins and gives me courage to live even when circumstances seem too hard to bear.

CHAPTER 19

THE PESTERING PETITIONER
Luke chapter 18

We may be sure that Jesus knew her name, this woman who had been deprived of her rights. She was a widow. It had been so easy for someone to take advantage of her. Maybe he had come to her in her need, offering his services as a benefactor. She was distraught by her husband's death, distracted, vulnerable. There were no lights flashing to warn her that this respectable gentleman was a predator, but now, here he was, declaring her to be in his debt.

Jesus not only knew her name. He knew that she had children too. It was only their suffering that drove her to such persistency. If it was she who was dragged away into slavery, maybe she would have suffered in silence, feeling that life had already lost its meaning and purpose for her. But she must fight for her boys. Already they were an oppressed people, under the iron heel of Rome, but that her children should be taken to serve one of their own race! This was something she need not, would not accept.

It was God, through his great Law-giver Moses, who had decreed that there should be judges appointed in every city, that the poor and oppressed might have the right of appeal. Justice must be done. She would go to the judge.

'It is no good you going to him. He'll never even agree to see you.' She would not listen to the advice of this pessimist. Of course she must go. He must listen to her. Right was on her side. She waited in the courtyard of the great house. How was it that some who had come in after her had already been invited inside and she was still waiting there? Never mind. She would come back tomorrow. She would not give up.

The next day was the same, and the next and the next.

'You won't get in to see him without the right connection,' she was told. 'If you bring a gift to this or that one, you might get somewhere.' But if she had money to offer as a bribe she would not be in the condition she was in. He must give her justice. It was his duty. That was why he was appointed as judge. She would see him. He must come out of his house at sometime.

'Sir! Sir! I beg of you, hear my case. Give me justice against my oppressor.' The judge was not best pleased to have his morning walk impeded by a woman throwing herself at his feet.

'This is not the time to state your case, woman,' he complained. 'You must come at the proper time and place.'

'Oh, sir,' she sobs, 'I have come and they wouldn't even let me in to see you. Sir, I beg you, let me tell you what happened,' but the proud man has ordered that she be pushed out of his way and he is walking on.

Now she knows the worst. It is not his corrupt servants who have been preventing her from coming before the judge. It was he himself, who should have been standing as God's representative, who is corrupt. What can she do? Where else can she go?

Is there a God in heaven that such things are allowed? She must believe that there is. Then for the sake of her children she must not give up. But to whom can she go? There is no one else.

Again she goes to the house of the judge. Again she is passed by as others come before him. Again she waylays this rich, heartless man whose only hope is to line his own pocket. She throws herself before him.

'Sir! Sir! My lands have been possessed, my children taken away into slavery. You are appointed to be the protector of the fatherless and the widow. Give me justice.'

Again she is pushed away. But this is getting embarrassing for the judge. He tries to find some other way through town but somehow the widow gets to know and she is there, begging, pleading.

He calls his secretary. 'Take down her details. Send a writ to her opponent. I'll hear the case tomorrow.'

The secretary's mouth drops open. There had been no bribe given, no pressure from some wealthy friend. This wasn't like his master.

Sheepishly his master explains. 'Yes, it is true that I am known as a man who neither fears God nor respects man, but I can't spend my life trying to avoid this persistent little widow. It is easier for me to settle her case and be rid of her.'

So it was done. Her sons and her land were restored to her. I am sure that she thanked the judge dutifully, but in her heart she knew that there was a God in heaven, a God who has promised to be a father to the fatherless and a husband to the widow, a God who had known the agony of her heart concerning her children and had heard her cry, and it was he first of all that she should thank.

Oh, it is only a parable, you say. Yes, but those who heard knew that there was many such a case in their land and so it is today. Jesus told this story because he knew and he cared.

There are millions in the world today who are oppressed, with no recourse to justice. There are many in positions of authority who have no concern for righteousness, but there is a God in heaven. He is righteous. He is good.

The widow woman was crying for her children. She had turned her face to heaven, believing that God was good. Then are we willing to cry to God, to be persistent in prayer for the many who are crying out day and night for help?

Jesus told this story about an unnamed widow woman because he wants us too to learn to be persistent, importunate in prayer. We may have to wait long for an answer. It may seem for a while that we go unheard, but we must persist, knowing that we come, not to an unjust judge, but to a God who is good, knowing, seeing and caring, the great Jehovah God. He will hear and answer.

CHAPTER 20

HARASSED HOUSE WIFE

What must she have felt like when her husband came home and told her that he had paid all their hard earned money to the inn keeper and he would get nothing in return?

Ah, now you are stretching your imagination, you will say. The Good Samaritan was not a real person. It is just a story that Jesus told.

But Jesus told it as if it were true. 'A certain man,' he relates, and with his knowledge of the hearts of all men we can be confident that he did not have to delve into the realm of fiction for the stories that he told. His hearers could all picture the certain man who went down from Jerusalem to Jericho. They had their share of entrepreneurs in those days, and the Jews have always been successful in business enterprise. Then of course, if you have money there is the possibility of being robbed, in some way or other. They all knew that travellers were taking the chance of being jumped by a gang of thieves on that lonely road, of being beaten up and left for the vultures to tidy up.

Probably they knew all too well the likelihood of the priest travelling the same road, and passing by on the other side, feeling himself too apart to get soiled with one so needy. They all understood that he felt his calling too high and holy for him to have contact with the rabble; and his holy garments: how could he risk getting them spoiled?

They would have identified more easily with the Levite who was really sorry and concerned for the poor fellow lying there. Yes, he could have passed on, presuming that he was dead. The only trouble was that he had stopped to look and realised that there was life in this one who had been beaten up. But the gang might still be around. He might end up in the same plight himself if he stopped to help him, and besides, he didn't have an animal to help to carry him. He could have given him water and bandaged him up a little, but then might he have been prolonging his misery?

Kinder just to leave him there and hope that death would be merciful and come quickly. We can all identify with the Levite, can't we?

But what about the Samaritan? 'A Samaritan who was travelling that way,' Jesus said. Was he going to or from the holy city? He would have been a brave man, risking the sneers and rejection of these superior Jews because he knew that they would not despise his wares if they thought they might have a bargain with him.

'You don't mean to tell me that you wasted our precious money on a Jew!' Can't you imagine his wife lashing him with her tongue as she found that not only had he used her precious housekeeping money, but that there were blood stains on his outer garment. As if that were not bad enough, his fine linen shirt had been torn where he had ripped off a strip to make a bandage.

'Do you think he will bother to seek you out in order to pay you back?' she sneers. 'You know how they despise us. He'll think it doesn't matter once he knows it was a Samaritan who helped him. And now how am I going to feed the children I would like to know?' Surely we are not stretching our imagination too far. It is so easy for the husband to be known as the generous one, handing out charity as he gets a burst of liberality; the husband who receives the praise, while it can be the wife who suffers and has to try to keep the family together.

And this unknown, despised Samaritan, answers her gently, for he can understand her frustration. 'I didn't expect him to pay me back. I didn't want that. But I am sure he will pass it on, and help others who are in distress.

'And don't worry, Wife. We have bread for today, haven't we? And look, I have a little money left. I am sure it was the good Lord who sent me along the road just then to help that poor fellow. He may have been a Jew, and I know they think that they are special to God, but I believe that our God is great enough to care about us too. We are all special to him, and he is no man's debtor. He will make it up to us, you'll see.'

I am sure that God did make it up them, as he always does, if not in kind, certainly in richness of blessing, so that even his poor frustrated wife, struggling to bring up her family, came to accept that her husband's generosity was not necessarily a bad thing.

If she had known that Jesus was going to relate that story, because he wants us all to be generous; to help the poor and needy; wants us to give when we can ill afford it so that we too may prove that God is no man's debtor and that he will give in return until we feel overwhelmed by his kindness.... Yes, if she had known, she would not have grumbled and scolded. But we wives have a very limited vision, and fearing that our husbands may be weak and susceptible, we may be inclined to grumble.

But we are only imagining. Perhaps it was not like this. Perhaps this Samaritan's wife did not scold her husband but instead quietly accepted her lot, labouring to get the blood stains from his cloak, patiently patching up his torn shirt, and lifting her heart to the good Lord who had prompted her husband to care for an unknown traveller, to meet their need. I hope that she understood that though he must have known that it would bring hardship to her and to the children, that he had felt that he had no choice because, as much as he knew of God, he loved him and so he had to love his neighbour too. Yes, I hope that she too was one of those wonderful wives who, though they may never have any recognition in this life, yet are content to live with their faces towards the sunrise.

CHAPTER 21

THE CANAANITE WOMAN
Matthew chapter 15

'Gentile dog!' She knew that that was what they must be thinking, and here she was, on the ground, grovelling yes, like a dog. She knew what those proud Jews thought of her. They wouldn't bother to give her a name. It was enough to know she was a Gentile, and a Canaanite at that. But she wouldn't have come unless she were desperate. Her only hope now was in this gentle Jew from Galilee.

We don't know how much she knew of her history, this Canaanite woman who had flung herself at the feet of the Saviour. She may not have know that hers was one of the tribes that the Israelites were supposed to have wiped out because God could no longer tolerate their evil ways. She might not have known that the Israelites were warned that if they allowed them to stay in the land that they would be like thorns in their sides. If she didn't know, she did know that they despised her and all of her tribe, and that it was easiest to keep as far away from these arrogant, self righteous people as she possibly could. She was quite content to live in this cosmopolitan community around Tyre and Sidon.

But now she was in need, and the only one who could help her was one of these proud Jews.

When she began to realise that her child was not like other children, we don't know. With a background of demon worship, it could have been that this child that she had longed for had never been normal. Did she have to shield her from the eyes of those who had come to offer their baby worship? She may have had a few months, even years of pleasure, delighting as her daughter took her first faltering steps, uttered her first endearing words, learned to play with the other children and to help her mother around the house. We don't know, but we do know that such tragedies can come unexpected and unexplained, and we know that at times the child that she had carried within her womb, welcomed and cherished, at times turned into an enemy, her dark eyes filled with hate, her tiny hands reaching out to claw and to destroy, her mouth filled with words that no child should have known.

Doubtless this mother had tried her own priests and witch doctors, but they could have been part of the cause and could only make matters worse. Nearly demented herself through grief and anxiety, what was it that first caused her to hope?

Did she marvel at some wayside flower and realise that such beauty could not be there by chance? Did she lift up her eyes to the snow clad mountains and become aware that though she was in such anguish, there must be some Goodness that had placed us in such a world. Not yet knowing him, did she cry out to God for help?

News of the Saviour must have reached even to that godless community. Good deeds speak far louder than words. They may not have known the message of this Carpenter from Galilee, but everyone was talking about the wonders that he performed, but what hope was there for her? He would never come to their district. Jews were not welcome there, even as they would be treated as outcasts if they strayed over their borders.

But come he had. When she felt that she was at the end of her tether after one of her child's violent outbursts she heard that Jesus had been seen in their coasts. Surely God had heard her cry. This must be the answer. She would take her daughter to him.

But the daughter would not co-operate. There was no way that she was going to be able to drag a screaming maniac through the streets. We can imagine her in some way seeking to restrain her and begging the unwilling neighbours to give an eye as she set out to find this healer.

She had no difficulty in knowing which one was Jesus, for he was dressed as a Jewish Rabbi. He had a bearing about him like none other.

'Lord, Son of David!' She had known how to address him. He must be the one in whom the Jews had set their hope. Somehow, seeing him, she had known that he could help her, and she must get help. She could go on no longer seeing her child suffering as she was, and she was suffering too. How often had she been ashamed to be seen on the streets because of her scars and bruises as she had sought to restrain her daughter. Of course she had no husband to help her. He had left her long ago, unable to share the pain and the shame.

'Lord, help me!' Again she had cried, trying to get nearer, but her cries were only attracting the attention of others to the presence of the Saviour and she seemed to be getting further away. 'Be quiet and go away,' one of Jesus' disciples had growled at her. 'Don't you know that the Master has come here to get away from all the attention?'

For one awful moment he had disappeared from sight and she had thought she had lost her opportunity, but then she had seen people crowding outside one of the houses. Jesus must be there. She would get in somehow. Pressing, pushing, wriggling, withstanding indignant elbows and hostile feet, she made it into the house, but there was no way that she would be able to stand before the Carpenter.

Were they trying to push her outside? In anguish she threw herself on the floor and wriggled her way to the very feet of the Saviour. A gentile dog - she was proving surely that she deserved the name. Here she was, grovelling on the floor. Would she be kicked aside? But her child was in torment. No matter what she suffered, she must get help. She reached out to touch his sandalled feet. 'Lord, have mercy on me.'

Lifting her head she looks into his eyes and knew that she did not need to speak further. He knew all that she had suffered, from the first moment when she realised that this was not her child who was behaving with such violence and hatred, but that some evil force was controlling her; he knew the resentment and misunderstanding of her neighbours; knew all the pain of the long years. He could kick her, call her a dog, but he must help her and heal her child.

One of the disciples is shaking her, trying to get her to go away. 'Don't you know that he has come for the people of Israel? He only came here to get out of the way for a bit because of all the hostility that has been stirred up?' But the woman will not go and the Master is speaking now.

'You must understand daughter. After all, it isn't right, is it, to take the children's food and give it to the dogs?'

She rises now from her prostrate position and kneels expectantly before him. She has heard the gentleness of his tone, seen the compassion in his look, and knows that he does not consider her a dog, a pariah, an outcast to be kicked and driven away, a scavenger only allowed to live because of its use in cleaning up the waste and rubbish. No, the word that he has used is of a pet dog, one that is loved and included in the family. It is Jesus himself who is giving her the confidence to claim her portion as she looks into his face and tells him, 'But the pet dogs are allowed to eat the crumbs that the children drop.'

We may be sure that that Canaanite woman walked home with her head held high. She did not need to rush to see whether what Jesus had said was true. She knew that her child was well. Never again would that evil spirit be allowed to torment them, or to fill their home with grief and fear. They might not be of the chosen race. They might be Gentile dogs in the eyes of men, but in God's sight they were precious. Had not God sent his Son into these border towns because he had heard her cry? They could live now, their faces towards the sunrise.

CHAPTER 22
THE UNNAMED DISCIPLE
Luke chapter 24

Who was this unnamed disciple who walked with Cleopas on that wonderful day of resurrection? It has been suggested that it was Luke, who as writer of the gospel would be diffident to include his name, but this cannot be for does he not state that he himself was not among the eye witnesses?

An unnamed disciple. We know that the beloved physician had regard for women, but even he might not have thought it necessary to include the name of Cleopas' wife. It could well have been she.

A disciple indeed, maybe she had not been free to travel around the country with Jesus and his followers. It is evident that their home had not been shut up for long. There is no mention of anyone else being with them at that solemn meal and yet they had been able to press the Lord to stay with them and food was soon put on the table.

Only eight miles or so from the city, she could well have accompanied her husband to the temple for the celebration of the Passover, and while there heard of the terrible tragedy that had befallen the Master. Jesus, the one in whom was all their hope, had been betrayed, arrested.

Could she have been there among the crowd who had bayed for Barabbas to be released and for Jesus to be crucified, her cry for the Saviour's deliverance going unheard? But no, maybe there were none of his followers there for his twelve close disciples had fled and the Pharisees had made sure that the many who loved him were not aroused. This deed of dread darkness had been under the cover of night.

But word had gone around. Had she been there when the terrible scourging took place? I hope not. How could any woman with a mother's heart have borne such pain, but she had heard of it. Yes, she knew. Surely she had joined the women of Jerusalem as they surged behind the cross that was being bumped so painfully over the cobbled stones. She would have seen his beautiful face so marred that she could hardly recognise the one who had taken her children into his arms, who had won the heart of her husband and brothers, and her own heart. She would have seen his back, scourged so that his flesh hung in ribbons, and heard his voice, ringing out in compassion in all his pain, 'Daughters of Jerusalem, weep not for me...'

Was she one who had stood around the cross, feeling that the darkness was an outward expression of what was engulfing her own heart, the shaking of the earth but an echo of that which was shaking her faith, for evil had triumphed and God and all goodness was dying on that cross.

She was glad that she had been there with her husband. At least she could encourage him to return to his home and take up again the life that he had left, maybe three years before. Hers had been the responsibility to keep the home together, only joining him on special occasions, but she had been a disciple none the less. They had been so sure that this one had been the Messiah, the one who would rout the enemy and restore to them David's throne.

Her limbs are aching, for who could have slept through those weary, endless days and nights when the Saviour lay in the grave? But she must place one foot in front of the other as they walked the dusty highway. There is nothing left but to return home. Nothing now to live for, but they must make an effort for the sake of their family.

Her husband walks in silence. She must get him to talk. That is the trouble with men. They bottle things up inside them and suffer all the more. At least she can help him by getting him to talk about all his hopes and fears, the terrible happenings that had come to pass to destroy all possibility of hope. Except for what the women had come to tell them, about the grave being empty! The pain and suffering must have affected their minds.

Somehow it does not seem an intrusion when the Stranger joins them. It must have seemed to her almost as if God had seen her desire to bring some sort of release to her husband by getting him to talk over these sad events and had sent someone to help her.

78

Oh, there is healing in talking about these things. Why, the Stranger is speaking now, talking about the scriptures that she had heard ever since as a child she was taken with her mother to sit in the women's section of the synagogue. She doesn't know when or how it happened but the heaviness has gone from her limbs. Her feet seem to be hardly touching the ground. She is aware now of the jubilation of the birds, the celebration of the wayside flowers. The whole of nature is declaring that the grave is not the victor, but that new life comes out of death.

The weight that had been as a stone in her breast has become a heart again, beating, responding, thrilling to the words of the Saviour, for though she does not yet know it, it was he who has come to walk with them and is opening up to them the Scriptures.

Before either of them have realised that the miles that could have seemed so long were behind them, they are back in Emmaus. He is leaving them, this one who has brought healing to their broken hearts, travelling on still further.

'O Sir, please, please spend the night with us. It will soon be dark. It is no trouble to prepare a meal.' Cleopas joins her in urging him to stay.

A little scurrying, and maybe some help from a neighbour and they are seated at their table, a simple meal set before them.

It was not Cleopas who asked the blessing and shared the bread. Jesus had accepted the place which is rightly his as Lord of our homes and our hearts and taking the bread in his nail scarred hands, blessing and breaking it, Luke records, 'their eyes were opened and they knew him.'

Their journey of perhaps eight miles had seemed so long when they had set out that morning, but now they flew over the road as they returned to Jerusalem to share the wonderful news with the other disciples. Everything is alright. Jesus is alive. The devil didn't win after all. God allowed all the pain and shame and tragedy because he will turn it all to good.

But they didn't need to say it, for Jesus was there, blessing them, giving them his peace.

How wonderful to have been that unnamed disciple who walked the road to Emmaus on that first Easter morning, and that was not the end of the wonder. Even if she had had to return home she would have heard of other wonderful appearances of the Saviour and undoubtedly would have gone with Cleopas to that appointed meeting in Galilee, watching with awe as her Lord was taken up into heaven, returning to his Father's heart and throne.

And wonder of all wonders, he had not left her, for through his Holy Spirit she could know him, still walking beside her, still speaking and opening to her the scriptures. Every day she could feel her heart warmed and know that experience of that first Easter day, when her heart had burned within her.

CHAPTER 23

JUST ONE OF THE WIDOWS
Acts chapter 9

Our hearts have all been saddened as we have heard of some ship lost at sea, but do we still remember the plight of the widows and children left behind? There were many such in Joppa. There usually are in any fishing port, and Joppa was no exception, for even the Mediterranean, which can be so blue and serene, can turn into a raging beast, ready to devour those who try to ride her. People would have been used to the sight of the women, their hands chapped and sore, eking out their pitiful existence by making or mending ropes or sail cloth, unloading the fish, or helping to carry the cargo from the larger vessels that had crossed the great sea to far flung lands.

They would have been used too to the sight of the ragged little children, playing tag between the nets that were hung out to dry when the weather was sunny and warm, but shivering in corners, begging piteously from the rich merchants when the winds were chill. Though they were still small, you might see them too, running to help to pull the boats up onto the beach or to carry the loads, hoping that they might be thrown a coin, or at least be given a basket of fish.

There would have been those among the widows who, finding their pitiful existence unbearable, would ply another trade among the sea-farers. We would like to think that the one of whom I write was not among those. She would have struggled to bring up her children to know some security or respectability, but who knows what we might do if we were in a situation where our children were starving, crying to be warmed and fed.

She was an Israelite. Did she go to the synagogue, segregated from the men yet nevertheless able to hear the scriptures read? Had she cried out for help to the God of Abraham, Isaac and Jacob; the God who had appeared to Hagar when her child was dying in the wilderness? We don't know, but we do know that one day her son came running home to show her his new little coat, snug and warm. 'A kind lady made it. She said I can keep it. And she is going to make one for Sarah too.'

We can imagine the relief of this mother as her children began to run expectantly to the shore each day to see this kind lady who had compassion on these fatherless children. They would be just as delighted when it was one of their friends who had a new coat, and besides, it was not just their little bodies for which she was caring.

'Dorcas, Dorcas, are you going to tell us a story about Jesus today?' She has crept up quietly with some of the other mothers. They stand in the shadows as they see their little ones settle quietly around this woman who had obviously never known any lack in her own life, and yet who cared for their children who were in such need. She is listening too as Dorcas told them the stories as best as she could remember, for she had never read them. They were stories that were passed from one to another, stories of one called Jesus, who had come and changed the lives of so many like themselves.

She was as anxious as her children to go now, this unnamed widow woman of Joppa, for little by little she had come to realise that though their situation was so sad, their lot so hard, there was a God who loved them. They were not without hope.

She would not have known of how inadequate Dorcas felt, nor of her longing that someone more gifted than she was, would come to Joppa to tell the glorious gospel, so that they might have a church as they did in other places with elders and teachers to care for the flock as men and women came to put their trust in Jesus Christ.

She only knew that here was a woman who loved them, who cared for their children and who made them feel that they were not just as flotsam and jetsam washed up on the shore, but that they too were special.

'Dorcas didn't come today, Mummy!'

'Perhaps she is busy. She will be there tomorrow.' But tomorrow came and no Dorcas. Then the news began to spread around. Dorcas is ill. She is very ill. She is dying.

'Why don't we ask Jesus to make her better?' Instead of their usual gathering on the sea shore they were crowding outside their benefactor's house. I'm sure it was one of the children who suggested it. Somehow a little one is so much quicker to realise that God is not just the God of history. We can picture the women and children there in the street, praying and weeping, being cautioned not to make a noise to disturb the patient, as one or another of her carers came out with a long sad face.

Then came the news, 'Peter is in Lydda. There was a man there who had been ill for many years and Peter prayed for him and now he is well and strong.'

They all had heard of Peter. Why, he had been in so many of the stories that Dorcas had told the children. He was one of the fishermen who had been with Jesus, helping him, one of his specially chosen followers. Surely he would pray for Dorcas and make her well again. Lydda wasn't so far away. They found two strong men who would stride along the coast road and bring Peter to them. They could not doubt that he would come.

'Aye! Aye!' There comes a wailing now from the upper room. 'It is too late. She is dead.' Our widow cannot help but join in the weeping, and yet hers was not the keening of desolation. 'Yes, go! Go!' she urges their chosen messengers as they hesitate.

'David, run home and bring that little coat that Dorcas made for you.' Somehow they had known that the sun was shining again when they had received those first little garments for their children. God is good. He loves you. This was the message they spoke.

The relatives are busy in the upper room, laying out the body, and preparing for the burial, but outside the widows are watching, sending their children to the outskirts of the town to see if the messengers are returning. At last the cry goes out, 'Peter is coming! Peter!'

They are all crowding around him now, weeping and showing him the little garments, all talking at once, trying to tell him of all Dorcas's acts of kindness, pushing their way with him into the room where their dear friend is laid out, ready for burial, but Peter raises his hand. His look is enough. They understand, and leave him alone with the body of their dear, dear friend.

Is there expectancy in her heart? Is she praying too as Peter, alone there with a corpse, kneels down and dares to pray in the name of Jesus that she would rise again?

A gasp, a cry and then a great song of praise and Peter comes to the door and - yes, Dorcas is there beside him.

Dorcas's prayer has been answered. An apostle has come to teach the people and lead many to place their faith in the Saviour. A church is established. Our widow is no longer a despised beggar woman. She has found herself accepted into a loving community and as her children grow she too is being trained in ministering to others. Through the love of one woman who was gifted in weaving and sewing she has found the riches of the kingdom of heaven. She too is living with her face toward the sunrise.

CHAPTER 24

SISTER OF A CELEBRITY
Acts chapter 23

It can never be easy to be the sibling of someone who achieves fame, while you remain a nobody; though perhaps in those days it was easier for a sister. Not expected to do exploits herself, she could find satisfaction in the prowess of her brother.

She would not even have been sent to school, this one who is unnamed, except as sister of the great apostle. Hers it was to learn the duties of housekeeping and home crafts; laws regarding foods that could be eaten, the way it was prepared, even the washing of pots. Always busy, there must have been a measure of longing as she saw her brother sent off to the synagogue school, coming home to show off his learning.

It would have been obvious even from those early days that her brother had outstanding talent. Soon they were leaving the city of Tarsus, with its affluence, its sea breezes and its cosmopolitan way of life to move to the stifling environs of Jerusalem. Her brother was in need of higher education and so the whole family was on the move.

I don't suppose she resented it. She must have shared the pride of the family as Saul was selected to study with the venerated scholar, Gamalial. He rose from one honour to another until, young as he was, he became a member of the ruling council of the Jews.

With such a prestigious brother it was inevitable that she should make a good marriage. Unable to read or write, only allowed into the synagogue as an observer, she was respected among the citizens of Jerusalem, and would have been proud to tell her children of their uncle.

Only now it seemed that her brother was achieving notoriety rather than fame.

Of course the followers of Jesus of Nazareth are deluded in believing that he has risen from the dead, but why does my brother have to go to such extremes, rounding them up, tearing families apart and committing them to prison and to death, we imagine her asking.

Then - 'Your brother has become one of them. He is preaching in Damascus that this Jesus is Lord and Christ.' She must have found it impossible to believe, but the rumours persisted. Then there was a long silence. Where was this brother around whom their lives had revolved? His career, once so promising, was shattered, and she and her family probably held in suspicion because of him.

Then she heard whispers of one, Paul, who was in Jerusalem, only it sounded as if it was one and the same as her brother Saul. Was it on this occasion when, held in suspicion by the Christians, as well as under threat of death from the Judaisers, that he visited his sister and told her of his life transforming experience on the road to Damascus?

It would have cost her if she were to admit to being of one mind with her brother, but whether an open disciple or not, I am sure that this sister would have prayed daily for Paul, and taught her children to do the same.

It must have been with relief that she heard that he had returned to their old home, Tarsus. He was settling down at last. A few years of quiet, but then the rumours began to spread again.

'Have you heard? Your brother, who used to be so devout, is not only preaching to those of other nations, but eating with them. To think of such infidelity!' I am sure that the family tried their best to deny, refusing to believe this gossip. If only she could hear from her brother's own lips that these things were not true. He had been brought up to observe the least detail of the law.

At last he came, not to deny but to explain. The good news of Jesus Christ was not for Jews alone, but for those of every nation. Paul made his defence before the council of apostles and amazingly they gave their blessing to what he was doing. Then they, his family, must accept it too. It was obvious that Paul, as they had come to call him, was being greatly used of God. Hadn't he had a word from the Lord that he would even stand before kings? He was certainly going into many lands.

'Mother! Mother! Tell us about Uncle Paul!' Her youngest longed for another visit from his uncle. He had been thrilled by Paul's stories of their journey to Cyprus and of the sorcerer stricken with blindness, of his shipwrecks and of the time when the people thought that he and Barnabas were Roman gods. He didn't like the part when the people turned against them and tried to kill them, but the story had had a happy ending.

'O Mother! Will he come for the festival this year?' They knew that Paul still loved the Jewish festivals, and Passover was extra special to him now he believed that Jesus was the true Passover lamb who had died for the sins of the world.

Paul's sister was probably praying that her brother would not come. There was an ugly mood among the Judaisers. They were so angry that Paul was welcoming the heathen into the kingdom of God that they had followed him around, stirring up opposition against him. Many a time his life had been in danger.

But he did come. Her joy was mixed with fear. 'Now don't go telling the neighbours that Paul is here,' she warned her family.

Paul already knew of the dangers. Hadn't the prophet taken his belt to act out his warning that he would be tied up and thrown into prison? Yes, he knew. He embraced them, praying for God to keep them in peace.

For a day or two everything seemed calm. Then came the terrible news.

'There was a lynching! They accused Paul of taking a Greek into the holy area of the temple. If the Romans hadn't come to quell the riot he would have been killed. As it is now he's a prisoner in the fortress.'

Can we imagine the agony of this sister? Was it in answer to her prayers that her son overheard the plot of the forty men who had taken a vow not to eat or drink until Paul was dead.

'I was on the roof, Mother, and I heard some whispering so I crept over to listen. They are going to ask for Paul to be brought before the council so that they can ambush him on the way and kill him.'

What could this sister do? A woman, she could not go herself, and it was her son who had heard of the plot. But how could she place him in danger?

A woman, yes, but one of courage and resourcefulness. Maybe she packed up a gift so that the lad could persuade the guards to allow him to visit his uncle, for we know that he did see him, and Paul in turn called for one of the guards to take his nephew to the chief captain so that he could tell him his story.

Those forty hungry, angry men, would never have known how it was that their plot did not succeed but Paul's sister knew.

It is doubtful whether she ever saw her brother again, but we may be sure that she prayed for him, when he was in prison, as bound with him, entering into his joys and his sorrows, meeting those who had come to trust in the Lord through him. Yes, she was just a sister, and no one bothered to record her name, but without her Paul's story might not have been completed.